3 9082 13713 2455

1/6/21

# Be the Parent, Please

W9-DGW-129

# BE THE PARENT, PLEASE

## STOP BANNING SEESAWS AND START BANNING SNAPCHAT

*Strategies for Solving
the Real Parenting Problems*

**Naomi Schaefer Riley**

TEMPLETON PRESS

Templeton Press
300 Conshohocken State Road, Suite 500
West Conshohocken, PA 19428
www.templetonpress.org

Designed and typeset by Gopa & Ted2, Inc.

Library of Congress Cataloging-in-Publication Data
Names: Riley, Naomi Schaefer, author.
Title: Be the parent, please : stop banning seesaws and start
banning Snapchat : strategies for solving the real parenting problems /
[Naomi Schaefer Riley].
Description: West Conshohocken, PA : Templeton Press, [2017] |
Includes bibliographical references. |
Identifiers: LCCN 2017039002 (print) | LCCN 2018027345 (ebook) |
ISBN 781599474830 (ebook) | ISBN 9781599475547 (pbk : alk. paper)
Subjects: LCSH: Technology and children. | Technology and youth. |
Child rearing. | Parenting.
Classification: LCC HQ784.T37 (ebook) | LCC HQ784.T37 R55 2017
(print) | DDC 649/.1—dc23

Printed in the United States of America

18  19  20  21  22     10  9  8  7  6  5  4  3  2  1

To Midge and Kay,

whose mothering and thoughts on mothering

are an inspiration.

■ ■ ■ ■ ■
■ ■ ■
■

# Contents

∎ ∎ ∎ ∎

# Acknowledgments

■ ■ ■ ■

I NEVER THOUGHT I would write a book about parenting—at least not until my kids were grown. It's like writing a memoir at the age of twenty-five. What do you know?

The answer would be not much—if I were to draw solely on my own experience. But while my children have made the questions surrounding technology more urgent in my mind, my own family cannot provide the answers. For those, I am grateful for the help of dozens and dozens of mothers and fathers around the country—old friends, recent acquaintances, colleagues, friends of friends. I hope you see your experience (if not your names) reflected in these pages.

I am also thankful for all the experts who took the time to speak with me—people who work in Silicon Valley, in Washington, and at universities around the country. This is a world I would not have understood without you. The input of so many teachers, principals, and caregivers has also enabled me to get a much broader view of the challenges that children and parents are experiencing today.

In terms of the structure and argument of the book, I would like to thank my editor, Susan Arellano, for her patience and feedback as well as Christine Rosen for her useful and encouraging comments.

My own experience as a mother has been made easier and better by my husband—a calm and steady voice of reason and love. Though we had different upbringings, our parents, I think it's fair to say, all came to the same conclusion—when raising kids, you can't pay too much attention to what everyone else thinks.

Though I'm sure I didn't appreciate it at the time, I owe a great debt to my mother and father for that lesson and so many others. They instilled in me a love for reading and writing that I hope to pass on to my children. Though they tell me they are relieved not to have to raise children today, it is hard to imagine grandparents with deeper devotion.

Lastly, I must thank Emily for her keen observations about human behavior; Simon for his curiosity about, well, everything; and Leah for her boundless enthusiasm for the world. Spending time with the three of you makes everything clearer and happier.

# BE THE PARENT, PLEASE

# Screen Time

■ ■ ■

I MADE IT two-and-a-half years into motherhood before my first trip to the emergency room. My daughter Emily had a cough that wouldn't let up that was now accompanied by wheezing. The squeaking noise under her breath was easy for me—a lifelong asthmatic—to recognize. So there we were, in a curtained-off area in the children's section of the emergency room. My husband was home with our younger son. Emily wasn't particularly upset, just tired and confused. And that's when I looked up and saw something mounted in the corner of the room—a television with *Dora the Explorer* bounding across the screen. It was the middle of the night in a strange place, but here was a familiar face.

Emily was immediately entranced and I was immediately relieved.

As I sat on the edge of her bed, memories of long evenings with my father in the emergency room came rushing back to me. I don't remember being afraid or uncomfortable— just bored. During each twelve-minute breathing treatment, I would count the animals on the wallpaper: How many giraffes? How many zebras? Why were all the rooms the same? Even when I was old enough to read, I couldn't focus on a book during these ordeals. And I didn't want to.

While we waited for what seemed like hours between

each time a doctor listened to my chest, my father would do anything to entertain me. There would be bad jokes, stories from his childhood, stories from his mother's childhood, and lessons about the American Revolution. As he blurred the line between stand-up comic and college professor, it never occurred to me what must be going on in his own head.

Only later when he would recount the story of my first asthma attack before the age of two, my face turning blue as he and my mother rushed me to the hospital, did I begin to understand how he was forced to mask his own fears. And how much easier it would have been to do that with a television on the wall tuned to a twenty-four-hour children's cartoon network.

In an instant, Dora relieved me of my job of making funny faces, of assuring Emily that everything would be fine, of lying to her that no one would need to stick her with a needle. The presence of that television allowed me to give the doctor my full attention and to speak to him without masking my concerns or changing the words to be more child friendly. Our night in the emergency room was long, but it could have been much longer.

There are so many occasions to be grateful that we live in the twenty-first century. And being in a hospital serves as a helpful reminder of all the advances that modern technology has brought us. Usually we think of antibiotics and X-ray machines and arthroscopic surgery. But the ability to distract us from pain, discomfort, and boredom is surely one of the greatest features of our technological age. For children with minor asthma attacks or with medical problems that are much more serious, we have learned to make time fly.

The truth, though, is that Dora and the rest of her friends on Nick Jr., PBS Kids, and the Disney Channel are not being broadcast late at night exclusively for the use of children's hospitals. There are all sorts of occasions when it is a relief for children to be occupied. And now it is easier than ever. We needn't depend on televisions, either. Our smartphones and tablets provide instant access to all of the shows, movies, and games our children could dream of. They can use these magical tools to draw, listen to music, compose music, take pictures, and make videos. Why try to retell the story of the Battle of Valley Forge? There are apps that enable you to relive the entire fight for American independence.

In her book *The Plug-In Drug: Television, Computers, and Family Life*, Marie Winn articulates the ways in which television has "transformed the experience of children's sickness for parents and children alike."[1] Published in 1977, the year I was born, Winn's description of parenting seems even more apt today than it did back then, particularly in the way that parents interact with sick kids: "Gone are the onerous requirements of time and patience on the parent's part—the endless story readings, the tedious card games . . . the listening to whiny complaints, the steady need to restrain impatience, to maintain sympathy, to act more lovingly than ever."[2]

But when adults are asked about their experiences with illness as children, they recall these times fondly. One woman told Winn what a treat it was that her mother took off from work when she was ill: "I remember the endless card games and cutting out pictures from magazines with her. I remember lying in bed and calling her to come and bring me this or that, again and again and again. And I remember how wonderful it felt, that she always came!"[3]

Winn notes that these memories often don't include any description of the illness or any actual symptoms and no one remembers scratching the chicken pox. But people do remember the unyielding devotion of their parents. This account made me feel guilty for all of the times I have allowed my sick children to plant themselves on the couch and watch PBS Kids from morning 'til night while I worked or cleaned the kitchen or caught up on the sleep I had missed the night before when I was holding them over the toilet while their father dutifully changed the sheets for the third time.

But I don't think occasionally using technology to distract our children makes us bad parents. It makes us human. Still, that doesn't excuse us from understanding the temptations that technology presents to us as mothers and fathers, the effects it has on our children, and the tradeoffs we are making when we give our children access to technology and technology access to our children.

There are so many forces pushing us to give our kids technology, including the technology companies themselves, our schools, our friends, and the culture at large. It's all happening so fast. One day we are wondering about whether an hour of *Sesame Street* is a good habit for a two-year-old, and the next minute it seems we have adolescents who won't look up from their phones long enough to have a conversation with us.

Screen time is getting away from us. Now is not the time for guilt about what we've done. It's time to take a deep breath and look at where we are, where our children are, and where we want our families to be.

## CHAPTER 1

# What We Don't Know Can Hurt Us

■ ■ ■ ■ ■

O N A SUMMER AFTERNOON recently, a friend and I started talking about screen time. Her boys, who ranged in age from ten to fourteen, were decent students. One was on a soccer team, two played musical instruments, and all enjoyed roaming around outdoors. But they really loved their computers. Their dad, a software engineer, had put together an elaborate desktop system for each child, complete with *Minecraft* and other games. The day I was visiting her, my friend was in a constant low-level battle to get them away from their screens. It was like watching her swat flies. As soon as she sent one child outside or got one to read a book, another would sneak on to a computer.

There was nothing unusual about the frequency with which her kids were looking at a screen, at least when compared with other American kids. A 2015 survey commissioned by Common Sense Media found that tweens (ages eight to twelve) are spending five hours and twelve minutes per day consuming digital media (not including listening to music and using screens at school or for homework). Teens (ages thirteen to eighteen), meanwhile, are spending about eight hours and twenty minutes on digital media each day.[1] A lot of parents are skeptical of these numbers when I reveal them, but other surveys have found the same thing. In 2010, the Kaiser Family Foundation actually found that kids from eight to eighteen are consuming more than eight-and-a-half hours of media per day—including listening to music on a device.[2]

But when parents stop to add it all up—the texting, the social media, the web surfing, the video games, the Netflix—they find the numbers less shocking. There is quite a bit of variation in these numbers. Teenagers whose parents had a college degree consumed slightly less than seven hours per day. Those from families with a higher income and who were white consumed less digital media than children from lower-income, less-educated minority homes.[3]

But let's assume that teens with all of the advantages in life are still spending upward of five hours on screens each day. What does that mean? Laura Vanderkam, who writes books about the way we manage our time, is fond of saying: "Time is a choice; 'I don't have time' means 'it's not a priority.'"[4]

When we think of all the things our kids don't seem to have a spare minute for—time to play outside, to see their friends, to read a book for pleasure, or to talk to a parent about their day—it is worth remembering that they are spending several hours a day watching videos, browsing websites, texting friends, and checking in on social media.

My friend was unsure about what could be done for her boys and their seemingly magnetic attraction to screens, or whether anything should be done. So she consulted her pediatrician: "How much time should my kids be online?" she asked.

"Well," he began, "there are no longitudinal studies on the effects of screen time so I really can't tell you."

It was an odd response, and not what she was expecting. But he is right. There are no studies of the long-term effects of what we now think of as screen time. It's weird to think that the iPad has only been around since 2010. There are studies of video games and studies of television, subjects to which we will return, but when it comes to social media, touchscreen technology, apps for small children, the effects of mobile devices on kids, or even texting, we don't have a good picture of how these things can alter learning, behavior, personality, or success in adulthood.

For some parents, perhaps that might bring a sense of comfort. Look, there's nothing to prove that technology is harming my child! But for most, it seems, the lack of information is only deepening the profound sense of unease that many parents have. It's the sense that we are all operating in the dark here.

Why did my friend ask her doctor about this subject? There was nothing ailing her children. They were exhibiting no signs of social problems or physical sickness. But parents don't know where to turn anymore for guidance about screen time.

In the fall of 2016, the American Academy of Pediatrics (AAP) came out with new recommendations for kids and screen time.[5] Children under eighteen months should completely avoid digital media, apart from Skype or apps that allow them to see and talk to Grandma in another state. Children from ages two to five should watch screens no more than an hour a day, which includes television programs, games on phones and tablets, and Netflix on the laptop. And even that hour should involve "coviewing," meaning parents should be sitting on the couch watching with their child.

For kids who are older, the AAP said that families had to set their own guidelines, but they made some priorities clear. Before kids look at a screen, they should have gone to school, done their homework, spent an hour doing some kind of physical activity, and socialized with family or friends. For young children, which the AAP recommends need between nine and twelve hours of sleep per day, this does not leave a lot of free time.

After the new recommendations appeared, a number of news outlets suggested that the AAP guidelines were now looser (because babies were allowed to Skype and some of the recommendations for older kids were left more to the discretion of families). "It doesn't make sense to make a blanket statement [for] screen time anymore," Yolanda Reid Chassiakos, a researcher at University of California Los Angeles and author of the new report, told CNN.[6]

But truth be told, if parents actually adhered to these recommendations, kids would be in much better shape. If twelve-year-olds, who got home from school at three or four in the afternoon, were required to play outside for an hour, do homework for another hour or two, and have dinner with their families before they could even pick up a tablet or phone for a few hours at eight in the evening with a firm ten o'clock bedtime, our children's consumption of media would look a lot different than it does now.

Yet very few parents are going to take these recommendations to heart. It's possible that pediatricians telling new mothers that they should not sit their first child in front of a television screen for too long may affect behavior, but if they don't make a real commitment to limit technology, the forces pushing them to hand over the phone are simply going to overwhelm whatever initial advice they received—certainly by the time the next child arrives. If these doctors wanted to have any impact on parent behavior, they should have been a lot more forceful.

Pediatricians could be allies in a war that parents know they're fighting. Instead, these doctors seem to be as weak-willed as the mom down the street who gives her eight-year-old a phone as a birthday present. In the war between you and the circular from Target with all the new video games coming out in time for Christmas, these doctors aren't doing enough to strengthen the resolve of parents. And it wouldn't be that hard.

After all, there is no doubt that mothers and fathers across the country are deeply worried and confused about how often and in what ways their kids should be using technology. Jenny Radesky, a pediatrician specializing in child development, recently tried to convene a focus group to see how parents were using technology with their kids. As Radesky remarks, the parents "treated this as support group instead. They thought it was so good to talk to other parents about this. They would say, 'I don't know what I'm doing. I don't know how to deal with this.'"

Radesky tells me that parents "perceive a lack of control over managing technology." For the lower-income parents, she said it "feels like this is a wave of newness they don't know how to approach. They want to be a good parent and get all this tech stuff." For many parents in the group, says Radesky, giving their kids devices was a "status symbol." And while they "worried about addiction," there was a "real internal tension." They wanted "their kid to master the technology, but then it was something they didn't know how to control."

While we don't understand exactly how this technology is affecting our children's lives, we know that it is. As parents, we notice things—little changes in our children's attitudes, their sleeping habits, their ability to focus in school. We see shifts in the ways they talk to us and interact with their friends. And we want to understand what is behind these changes.

We have suspicions about what's going on because, honestly, we see these little differences in ourselves as well. We see how technology has made our lives both more convenient and more frenetic. We've seen how we are only half-involved in our conversations with other people. But we are much more accustomed to and perhaps comfortable with scrutinizing our children than ourselves—and so all this is easier to see in them.

Attentive parents have always tried to discern what is shifting their children's behavior and considered ways to fix it. Maybe they are eating too close to bedtime and having trouble falling asleep. Maybe their friends are teasing them so they don't want to go to school in the morning. Parents cannot solve everything that is wrong with their kids' lives, but until recently they had some sense of how different activities influenced them and what to try differently if things were going south. To be happy and healthy, most kids need to eat well, sleep well, exercise, get some intellectual stimulation, and have friends.

Technology is the X factor. Is it good or bad? Do our kids need it? Or do they just want it?

. . . .

As parents, part of our unease comes from realizing that technology has made our children's lives fundamentally different from our own childhoods. And I don't mean some idyllic 1950s family. I mean the childhoods of people who are parenting today. What has changed? For those of us who were children in the 1970s or 1980s, screens were certainly available. Indeed, as kids we probably had more unsupervised access to television. Our parents gave us more freedom to be alone after school, and some kids used that freedom to watch TV.

But what did we watch? When I was eleven, I came home after school every day to an empty house by about two fifteen. With little homework and no supervision, the world was my oyster. And I proceeded to watch soap operas—specifically a show called *Santa Barbara*. Some of it was not appropriate; some of it went right over my head. The assumption of television executives and advertisers was that the only people watching television then were adults or toddlers at home with their mothers. I could have watched cartoons or even MTV, but this was an era when racy music videos were relegated to moments after my parents were home, and often after my bedtime.

Compare this to the array of options that a child home at this hour might have today. Whether your children have a penchant for rap videos, violent movies, or just tween sitcoms, there is something for everyone.

Video game systems certainly provided some after-school and weekend entertainment when I was younger. But is it even worth comparing *Tetris* and *Mario Bros.* to *Call of Duty* or *Grand Theft Auto*? It's not only the content that seems foreign to thirty- and forty-something parents. It's also the time. How many of my friends spent more than a couple of hours a day on a Nintendo system or at an arcade? Today, your children could let an entire afternoon and most of the night go by playing *Minecraft* or something more disturbing if you didn't cut them off.

Kids are on screen for so much time, and we don't know what the effects are. Parents are hungry for guidance. Are they supposed to believe science writer Steven Johnson that *Everything Bad Is Good for You*? Will playing more video games give our children better hand-eye coordination and turn them into more skilled Air Force pilots? Or should they believe psychotherapist Nicholas Kardaras's opinion that *Screen Addiction Is Hijacking Our Kids*? Will being on the screen more turn our children into sickly drones whom we won't recognize in a few years?

Television is the easiest place to start answering the questions about the effects of screen time. The literature is vast, but after talking to numerous researchers, it's clear that something of a consensus has emerged.

Tim J. Smith is the principal investigator of the Tablet

Project, a research center based at Birkbeck University and King's College London, which is devoted to studying the effects of touchscreen devices on the cognitive, brain, and social development of infants and toddlers. Before he began looking into the question of tablets, he had to understand what came before them.

"Because television has been around for sixty-plus years, there have been longitudinal studies." Smith notes that television "seems to have an independent contribution to various negative outcomes for children, including language delay, poor physical health and possible delinquency, and later criminal behavior." Many of the early studies conducted on television and children failed to account for certain factors associated with families that watch a significant amount of TV. In these families, children are less likely to be physically active, more likely to be eating food that's bad for them, less likely to have parents who speak to them a lot and in ways that develop their language, and more likely to be exposed to other factors that lead to delinquency. But the studies since then have controlled for these environmental factors. And now the impact is clear.

Research also suggests that it is not just time spent staring at a television that influences outcomes for kids. It's also television as background noise. Heather Kirkorian, who runs the Cognitive Development and Media Research Lab at the University of Wisconsin, has written a number of papers on the effects on children of television that is simply on in the home for several hours a day. Even if the mother is "watching the news while the baby is playing, we find generally negative effects. The kids are distracted from play and the parents are distracted from social interactions with their kids."[7] Not surprisingly, Kirkorian tells me, she and her colleagues have found that "more hours of background television in the home negatively predicts cognitive abilities for kids at four years of age."

But what about the content? Large-scale longitudinal studies suggest that children who watch more violent television are more likely to engage in aggressive behavior as adults. A 1972 study followed children from age eight to age nineteen and controlled for the participants' initial aggressiveness, social class, and IQ. Among boys, watching a lot of TV violence at age eight predicted peer reports of violent behavior at age nineteen.[8] A 2003 study of five hundred individuals over fifteen years followed children from the first or third grades into their early to mid-twenties. Controlling for variables like parental aggression as well as early IQ and social class, it found that heavy exposure to TV violence in childhood predicted increased self-reported physically aggressive behavior in adulthood for both boys and girls.[9]

Just as there is evidence that watching violent television can lead to more aggressive behavior among some children, there is also evidence that this is the case for kids who play violent video games. A meta-analysis of research about video game violence included a dozen studies and 4,526 participants. Researchers found a small but positive relationship between the amount of time spent playing violent video games and later violent behavior.[10]

None of this means that all or even most kids who watch violent television will behave violently. Indeed, as some experts point out, as our video games have become more violent, our society seems to have become less so. But those are overall trends. These studies suggest that excessive exposure to television violence makes violent behavior in individuals somewhat more likely.

Conversely, educational television can also have a mildly positive effect on children's development. Longitudinal studies suggest that exposure to programs like *Sesame Street* or *Blue's Clues* or *Mr. Rogers' Neighborhood* can aid children's development of vocabulary and social skills.[11] Generally speaking, these effects were observed among kids in disadvantaged homes. Perhaps not surprisingly, it was better for them to be watching *Sesame Street* than to have little adult interaction or negative interactions with adults. One study even suggested that *Sesame Street* was a more effective intervention with these kids than the early childhood program Head Start.[12]

But for these effects to be felt in any significant way, kids need to be watching these programs with adults who are interacting with them. In an article in the *Journal of Children and Media*, researchers at Texas Tech and the University of Oregon reported the results of a study on 127 preschoolers who watched episodes of the cartoon *Daniel Tiger's Neighborhood* (a spin-off of *Mister Rogers' Neighborhood*). They found that watching the show "was associated with higher levels of empathy, but only for preschoolers" whose parents interacted with them in productive ways about the show.[13]

The study's authors note that parents who want to see these effects are supposed to sit with their children during the show and "try to help your child integrate what they learn . . . into their own life," "ask your child questions about what they are watching," "repeat dialogue your child heard," "point out the good things that characters do," "tell your child that you agree with the message," "encourage your child to imitate the behavior of characters," and so on.[14]

This is quite a big caveat. Most parents do not use television in this way. More likely, they are turning on *Daniel Tiger* as a distraction so that they can get something done without children interrupting. But as parents, we shouldn't fool ourselves into thinking our kids are getting much out of these shows without our input. Rachel Barr, a professor of psychology at Georgetown University, says that "just as you wouldn't expect a fifteen-month-old to be able to know what a book means on their own, you shouldn't expect them to do it with a screen either."

But surely, the popular assumption goes, games are better for kids than televisions because they're more interactive. Indeed, there have been large-scale studies that suggest there are improvements in spatial recognition and reasoning that come from playing video games. Even infants and toddlers who swipe on screens were found to have better small motor skills than those who didn't. Researchers at Temple University and Northwestern University reviewed 217 research studies on educational interventions using video games and found that "people of all ages can improve at all types of spatial skills through training, period," as principal investigator Nora Newcombe explains.[15] Their evidence not only shows that the skills improved but also that the subjects were able to translate these new skills into real-world settings.

But at what cost? As Tim Smith of the Tablet Project notes, the data on whether there is a real cognitive benefit to being a gamer is "mixed." He states, "Those kids spending time playing games are trading off other activities." Indeed, in one study he cites, parents of kids who were planning to buy their children video game consoles were divided into two groups. Half of them were asked to hold off on the purchase for six months. Explains Smith, "The students who got the console decreased in academic performance and had more behavioral problems" than those who didn't. It might be that the games altered the children's brains in some fundamental way, but the more obvious explanation is simply that the games were a distraction and that the kids wanted to play them so badly that they were acting up in order to use them more.

Given what we know about the effects of television and video games, there is plenty of reason to be skeptical even at this early stage about the effects of touchscreen games on phones and tablets. And some parallels are already clear. For instance, just as background television noise seems to be distracting caregivers from speaking and interacting with children, the use of mobile devices seems to be doing the same. A study in the journal *Child Development* found that children of parents who were distracted by their phones exhibited more behavioral problems than the children of parents who were not distracted as often.[16] Anyone who has watched parents at the playground in recent years will not find this surprising.

Jenny Radesky, who is based at C. S. Mott Children's Hospital in Michigan, spent time studying the interaction of parents and children at fast-food restaurants.[17] Not only were parents on their phones more distracted and less likely to interact with their children, they were also more likely to be short-tempered. She and her team also looked at mothers who were feeding their babies in high chairs—something that adults often find boring. When they were checking their phones at the same time, they were less likely to be speaking to the babies. Radesky wonders whether this is cause or effect: "Are they trying to withdraw on the phone? Or is there something that's coming from the device and changing interactions with kids?" She posits that "both are probably happening."

And what about the kids themselves? For small kids, "interactive features can help or hinder learning," says the University of Wisconsin's Heather Kirkorian. Looking at children between the ages of two and five, she has found that many kids learn more from watching someone else play a game on a screen than when the kids do it themselves. She speculates that often the games we give to kids to get them to learn things can actually make it harder for them to learn. First the child has to figure out how the technology of the game works, and then he or she has to figure out the content.

In her own work with infants and toddlers, Rachel Barr of Georgetown University has found that a parent's presence can more than double the chances that a child figures out a task on a touchscreen, and a parent who is "warm and responsive and sensitive and uses clear language" can increase the likelihood of success even more. Just like educational television's benefits are felt mostly as a result of adult presence and interaction, the same is true with touchscreens. But this does not reflect reality. Just as most adults are not sitting down on the couch with their children to watch *Daniel Tiger*, most parents are not using screens as a way to interact with their children.

■ ■ ■ ■

If you ask parents about when they let their kids have screen time, the first reason most of them offer is travel. "When you're hurtling across the country in a metal tube at five hundred miles an hour, pretty much anything goes," one mother of two toddlers with family living on the opposite coast told me. And who can blame her? Every few months there is a blog war about screaming children on airplanes. Should the other passengers be more tolerant of crying babies? Should parents be better at calming them? Kind parents give out goody bags with earplugs for passengers nearby. Business travelers hoping to sleep on long flights don't get a moment's peace. Inside of the speeding metal tube there is little room for compromise. But there are screens.

There are only so many hours in a day and only so many years in a childhood. And when those hours and days and years are made to "fly by"—even in an effort to reduce discomfort and boredom—something can get lost in the process.

I don't want to sound like one of those ladies in line at the supermarket telling the mother with a screaming toddler that she should "enjoy these years"—Lord knows I've been tempted to hand them my bickering children and head for the parking lot! But parenthood is all about keeping things in perspective, and many of us are losing it.

Our first long flight with Emily, our first child, was when she was eighteen months old. We were on an airline that offered a video console on the seatback with a handheld controller you could pull toward you. Emily would have been perfectly happy to press all the buttons for the six hours we were in the air, but the controller also included the button to call the flight attendant. "Look," I explained, "I can take this thing away from her and she will scream mercilessly. Or you can just ignore our calls for the next six hours. Your choice."

Travel by car is not much better, though at least it doesn't involve innocent bystanders. The best you can hope for is a long nap. But more often, children strapped mercilessly into car seats for long periods of time will just keep asking, "Are we there yet?" And those are the ones rational enough to speak. On one four-hour car trip, my rear-facing eight-month-old was unsatisfied with the music available on the CD player and screamed consistently unless I actually sang "Baby Beluga."

## Tips for Cutting Back

Skip the screens for short trips. Yes, there's a good reason to give a child a device when you're in a metal tube traveling across the country at five hundred miles per hour with two hundred other people. The same is not true of a trip to the supermarket.

Parenting can seem like one long exercise in frustration. In fact, despite all the advances of modernity, parenting is possibly more frustrating than ever. Sure we have gliders and wipe warmers and exersaucers. But none of those really makes much of a dent in the boredom, discomfort, and irritation that children feel when we force them to do things they don't want to.

Some of those things that seem normal today would have been considered absurd a hundred years ago. There was a time when one was not expected to travel for every holiday and when children mostly stayed in a close radius of their homes. We tend to think of previous eras as a time when children were better behaved. And certainly there was stricter discipline. But two-year-olds were not expected to sit in high chairs and keep their composure through several courses of a meal. They ate separately. Our ancestors didn't have battles over whether the parents of loud children should be made to leave shows or restaurants because no one would ever bring a child to one in the first place. It's no wonder that in our desperation to find ways to entertain them and keep them quiet, we have resorted to giving them our phones at every opportunity.

In so many ways, we are forcing children to live in an adult world. It's not only that they attend events and visit places previously reserved for adults. Children used to have a specific dress code that would define them as children. Now the clothes they wear are just miniature versions of adult items. They are keeping hours close to their parents. One mother told me that her own mother would send her and her siblings to bed by eight when they were well into their teens just so that her parents could have time to themselves. Now our kids are invited to bar mitzvahs that end after midnight and we expect our high school kids will put us to bed every weekend. And we have greatly expanded the topics and language we consider appropriate for children as well.

As Kay Hymowitz noted in her book *Ready or Not: Why Treating Children as Small Adults Endangers Their Future—and Ours*,[18] we have determined that children as young as eight are capable of emotional maturity. We have offered them the independence to make decisions for themselves about everything from their friendships to bedtimes, and the results have not been pretty.

We have failed to make a distinction between the knowledge and responsibilities of children and adults. At the same time, though, people complain that our young adults seem to be coddled, infantilized even. This may be because we treat our children inconsistently. On one hand, they are like little treasures who cannot participate in games where trophies are only given to the winning side, and on the other hand, we act like they are fully formed beings—our peers even—who understand all of life's most difficult lessons.

To understand how we have arrived at this point, it is necessary to look at the total shift in the nature of parenting that occurred in the second half of the twentieth century.

In her best-selling book, *All Joy and No Fun*, Jennifer Senior describes it perfectly: "Today parents pour more capital—both emotional and literal—into their children than ever before, and they're spending longer, more concentrated hours with their children than they did when the workday ended at five o'clock and the vast majority of women still stayed home."[19]

It used to be that the kids poured the capital. The twentieth century marked the first time in human history that having children didn't increase your economic standing. Raising more able-bodied boys and even girls used to mean that more people in your household could bring in income. And since child mortality rates were so high, the goal was to have more

kids because you didn't know how many of them would survive to adulthood.

But now we live in an era where children are an expense, a
luxury even. We are having fewer of them and investing more
in each one, buying them nice clothes and good educations in
the hopes that they will reflect well on us and carry forward
our ambitions and values after we are gone.

But, as Senior writes, the goals of parenting today "are far
from clear. . . . Because children are now deemed emotionally
precious, today's parents are also charged with the psychological well-being of their sons and daughters, which on the
face of it may seem like a laudable goal. But it's a murky one,
and not necessarily realistic: building confidence in children
is not the same as teaching them to read or change a tire on
your car."[20]

Even if you have figured out what it means to raise a child
successfully or raise a successful child (which may be different things), more than likely parenting will be very tedious
at times.

Just think about life before children. (I know, it's hard to
remember sometimes.) For middle-class parents, their exis-
tence prior to having kids revolved around work and friends.
Even if your job was not the most scintillating, you could get
through it and meet your friends for drinks afterward.

And during the workday, you might have at least achieved
what we now refer to as "flow." A term popularized by psychologist Mihaly Csikszentmihalyi, flow is that blissful state
where you are so engrossed in the task at hand that you don't
notice time passing. It can be achieved by playing music or
entering numbers into a spreadsheet. I spent one summer
working as a bank teller. At the busy branches, with a steady
stream of customers, the day flew by—not because there was
anything particularly interesting about filling out deposit

slips. Despite how lovely it sounds, there's nothing inherently worthwhile in achieving flow. But it can be a kind of pleasant state in which things seem to be moving along well.

It is nearly impossible to be in this state when caring for a small child. As Senior observed, this is at least in part because your attention is constantly being refocused as your child changes moods and activities. You're in the middle of your pretend tea party that's taken ten minutes to set up, when suddenly your child wants to go find her left slipper. Or she has to go to the bathroom. Or you can see that she has to go to the bathroom, but she denies it. So you will spend the next three minutes arguing about it until the doorbell rings and she starts demanding a snack while you're negotiating with the electrician. In so many ways it is more worthwhile to spend the time with your child than to enter numbers on a spreadsheet, but there comes a moment in the day of a parent where you long for the spreadsheet.

A friend of mine who married and became a full-time stay-at-home mother of three once described to me the change in her life after she left work as a magazine editor. "You know how you have lists, Naomi?" I laughed. When we were fresh out of college, we used to keep neat pages of tasks, both personal and professional, that had to be accomplished each day or each week. "Well," she continued, "I start each day with a list. And nothing ever gets crossed off."

Thankfully, as her kids got older, my friend was able to do more—she is a writer and choreographer and has even experimented with homeschooling—but she still struggles with completing tasks at hand. One of the reasons that it is hard for parents (mothers especially) to go back and forth between caring for children and working is that work has lists. Progress, in some form or another, can be measured. Even the best, most organized mother may find that nothing gets crossed off the list on a particular day spent with her children. And her children may actually be better off for it. But you won't ever know for sure.

It's not just hard for us super-organized, overeducated types to adjust to the rhythms of toddlers. As Americans put off marriage longer and longer, we get used to being only with adults. We have smaller families, and unless we are specifically employed to babysit or work as a counselor at summer camp, it is easy to go years, even decades, without spending much time around small children. It is easy to forget how different it can be. It is easy to lose track of the distinction between children and adults, and that may be one reason why we start to treat our children as our friends and talk to them like adults.

Moreover, for twenty- and thirty-somethings used to an active social life, the initial stages of parenthood can be a deeply isolating experience. Sure, everyone loves to talk about going to "mommy and me" groups, having baby play dates, and drinking wine at the park while your kids are going down the slide, but the truth is these are reactions to the fundamental loneliness that many new parents feel. A friend of mine whose daughter was born several weeks premature pined for the day the doctor told her it was safe for the baby to attend a music class—just so she could go somewhere besides the supermarket.

Our families have been shrinking since the 1950s, which means that most young adults having children today do not have more than one sibling. And they're probably living farther away from the family they do have. So your mother or your sister or your aunt is not going to pop by unannounced to have coffee while you're giving the baby some tummy time. By contrast, my grandparents didn't have to wait for such moments at all when raising their children. My mother and her brother grew up with their parents, their aunt, and their grandmother all living in the same Brooklyn apartment. Things may have been crowded, but they were not lonely.

These days, the neighbors will not be popping by, either. Of course there are exceptions, but most blocks aren't teeming with stay-at-home mothers waiting for you to come running in with your latest "Is this normal?" question about the toddler. (Which is one reason, I suspect, that pediatricians' offices have become hotlines for hysterical mothers asking what seem to some nurses I've talked to like inane questions.)

When my children were born, I was not living near family, but I do remember being grateful to have a schoolteacher living next door. When my son did a face plant on our sidewalk and I saw blood gushing from his lip, I ran next door. The calm teacher (and mother of three) handed him a cherry ice pop and told me to sit down at her kitchen table and relax.

Most days, though, unless I sat myself on the front stoop, I could go without adult interaction from four in the afternoon to nine at night, when my husband arrived home. Despite going into an office two days a week, it was still a rough transition. When my oldest was a baby, I'd sit on the floor with her for hours each evening, talking, singing, making faces—even before she could respond in any meaningful way. It can be exhausting trying to make conversation with someone who doesn't talk back.

There were nights when I would pine for the moment it was time for her to watch a half-hour Elmo video. I may have looked forward to it more than she did. I wondered what would happen if I let her start watching earlier. But it was a line in the sand I had drawn for us.

Was there something wrong with me? Of course I loved lying on the floor with her and making a funny noise each time she honked my nose. But there were nights I felt like I was performing in a one-woman show. Some parents find that these activities come naturally—it is no effort to turn the thoughts in their head into a one-sided conversation with a baby. I was not among them.

But that did not matter. Like educated parents today, I am acutely aware of all the research on how talking to your children constantly and from a very young age can make a huge difference in their intellectual and social development.

The quantity of words a child hears each day directly correlates with the growth in his or her vocabulary and IQ. Researchers have found greater language and intellectual abilities in children who heard more modifying words (adjectives, adverbs) and more verbs in different tenses. This is also true of kids who got to hold conversations on subjects of their own choice. While these often turn out to be the most entertaining conversations with children, they also require the most patience. It takes kids a while to find the words they're looking for and to pronounce them in a way adults can understand. And often the whole point of the story is buried under multiple layers of completely irrelevant information.

If you want to know why parents are constantly hovering over their children, it's not just simply out of fear that junior will get a scrape on the playground. It's also to make sure he's heard fifty thousand words by age two. Otherwise, he won't get into a good college and will be doomed to a life of menial labor. At which point his parents will be deemed failures.

When we changed the goals of parenting—from raising small people to help on the family farm to raising receptacles for all our hopes and dreams—we also changed the methods of parenting. Perhaps without noticing, our parenting strategies evolved to be more geared toward ensuring our children are never bored, uncomfortable, or at the slightest disadvantage when compared with their peers. By many measures, though, we are failing to prepare them for life as independent adults.

Children's expectations also contribute to these traps of modern parenting, forcing all of us to lose sense. A typical Facebook post from an acquaintance, a working mom, comes to mind. She posted a picture of a Playmobil set and wrote: "After being up for 13 hours, working, taking care of kids, and making a nice family dinner (but before cleaning it all up). . . . Six-year-old son: 'Mom, can you put this together? It's just a few pieces.'" A reasonable observer could have come up with any number of responses to this query: "Maybe tomorrow." "Why don't you start it yourself and see how far you get?" "Ask your father." But out of some bizarre sense of guilt, loyalty, or obligation, this mother had an entirely different reaction. The next morning, she posted this: "That's right, folks. I did it. 156 pieces. 3 hours. Grrrr. . . . @Playmobile."

I don't mean to pick on this particular mother. Who among us hasn't spent hours trying to follow inscrutable assembly directions for kids' toys? But this was actually a toy that the child was supposed to build. And if the child couldn't even attempt to do this on his own, then it was not the toy for him. The line between helping kids and doing things for them is consistently blurred. And why not? It's so tempting. When we do it for them, it's faster, it's better, it's neater. Whether it's math homework or college application essays, if the goal is to give your kids the edge, taking over the project yourself is the obvious solution.

But the effect of all this hovering over our kids, protecting them from getting things wrong, shielding them from frustration, and stopping them before they fail is turning them into creatures that other adults can't work with, let alone deal with.

It's not just parenting that has changed. It's economics. There are many things that have grown more expensive relative to our salaries, not least of which is housing. But toys and clothing have gotten much cheaper.

You can outfit a toddler for an entire year at Old Navy for a few hundred dollars. And if you want to see the difference in how cheap toys have become relative to income, just check out the goodie bags kids receive at birthday parties. I remember getting a couple of pieces of candy and a noisemaker. My children come home with bags of plastic gadgets from Oriental Trading. Or a hardcover book. Or a baseball cap. Or a board game. Or a small Lego set.

Especially when kids are small, parents often don't have financial reasons to deny them what they want. Sure, there are lots of things that families want but can't afford—a bigger house, a nicer neighborhood, better schools, more exotic vacations, more time off from work—but a new sweater or doll or game is not going to break the family budget.

Middle-class parents have to manufacture reasons to say no to their kids. In his book *The Opposite of Spoiled*, *New York Times* finance columnist Ron Lieber notes that kids who are far from rich can still be spoiled. Not just because they always get their way; but because lavishing them with possessions can be easily accomplished depending on how many relatives dote on a child.[21]

The only thing standing between kids and their immediate gratification is their parents. It's not an easy position to be in. In December 2015, when the hot Christmas gift was the Hoverboard, a doctor wrote in to Lieber asking how he could tell his son that even though the boy had saved up the hundreds of dollars necessary for the hot new mode of transportation, the parents felt it was "over the top" and didn't want him to get one. In another era, in another family, the answer could have been that it was outrageously expensive—that's why. But for this family, which had already helped the boy purchase an iPhone, the new toy was hardly out of reach.

It is not only that most toys have become cheaper, it is also that everything is immediately available. It's an odd thing now to watch *The Music Man* and see kids waiting anxiously for the Wells Fargo wagon to bring them items ordered from the Sears Roebuck and Company catalog months earlier. Today, thanks to Amazon Prime, any product that takes longer than two days to arrive makes my kids wonder if the UPS guy is sick.

Whether it's entirely accurate or not, our kids have the feeling that everything is in reach financially and available immediately. Whether it's movies on Netflix or songs on iTunes, immediate gratification is the order of the day.

But as anyone who has experienced adulthood knows, successfully navigating the world of work and relationships requires the delay of gratification. How can parents teach their kids to pass the proverbial marshmallow test in a world where all you have to do is press a button and it seems like marshmallows fall from the sky? Or at least from drones.

In the modern world, parents are often the only barrier between their children and every sort of information, entertainment, and gratification. When there was only a single TV at home, only a few channels, and very little programming specifically for children, it was easier to say no. Children weren't demanding to watch the evening news in most cases.

But today it seems like our lives are full of opportunities to make exceptions. When the line at airport security is too long, when the restaurant is not making kids' meals fast enough, when there is traffic getting home from school, when our bosses demand that we work in the evening or over the weekend, it is easy to justify pulling out phones or tablets to babysit our children. Sure we have rules in place that they can only have a certain number of hours of screen time per day or per week, but this is an emergency. Or maybe not an emergency, but a tough spot.

Once kids realize the possibility is there—that there's a chance you will take out the iPad in the middle of the day—then it becomes a constant source of tension. Under what other circumstances might you do the same thing? Our kids are constantly testing us to see what other exceptions can be carved out. There's a similar dynamic with food. In a widely read rant in the *Washington Post*, Amanda Kolson Hurley wrote about our culture of "snackism": "We cave to our kids' snack requests, even before meals. . . . We walk around with trail mix and Sun Chips stuffed in our bags like we're mobile, no-fee vending machines. We schedule snack time into every group activity, drawing up elaborate rosters and dictating which foods meet our collective nutritional standards." Half of American kids, she notes, snack four times a day.[22]

Our inability to tell kids that they will have to wait until we get home, until the next meal, until we are seated at a table with our family is, at bottom, a desire to make sure they are never uncomfortable, never less than fully sated. We have a deep-seated fear that we will be in line at the grocery store, at a doctor's office, in a traffic jam, and the kids will get hungry and . . . well . . . who knows what? But as with technology, once everyone realizes the snacks are in the diaper bag or in the car, no child will want to wait for an all-out emergency before asking for them.

Before parents carried snacks everywhere, kids somehow managed to survive. And before the proliferation of on-demand technology, there were other options for keeping kids busy while we worked or cleaned or had some alone time. For one thing, there were other kids readily available. Children had more siblings, of course. But there were also just more kids hanging out in the neighborhood. Now, of course, they are all busy with after-school activities or prescheduled play dates.

Other things have changed too. For some families it is dangerous for kids to play outside by themselves. And it is easier to monitor children while they are inside than wandering around a neighborhood. Statistics show, though, that on the whole, children are actually safer than they were in, say, the 1970s. Crime is down overall. Violent crime is also down. And physical assaults against children are down, too—33 percent just between 2003 and 2011.[23]

Still we are worried, and technology helps alleviate our fears. And it means our children won't always be demanding more independence. It is a babysitter. It can provide respite for harried parents at the end of the day—whether they have been at work or at home. It is tidy. When the kids are finally in bed, none of us wants to walk around the house cleaning up art supplies or Legos or doll accessories. The iPad, on the other hand, just needs to be recharged.

And what about the educational benefits of these devices? It's not all violent (*Grand Theft Auto*) or mindless (*Candy Crush*). Many kids aren't using these screens to watch cartoons on Netflix. It's a lot easier to justify giving your four-year-old an iPad if every once in a while they'll learn something from it too.

Their teachers seem to approve. Kids come home from school with assignments to do on the computer—math drills or vocabulary "quizlets." What could be so bad about time spent on the screen if it means that kids enjoy learning more? And besides, they're so good at figuring this stuff out. How do they already know what buttons to press at the age of two?

Our friends, our communities, our institutions—everything seems to be pushing us to give kids more time with screens, not less. Our culture, our economic system, and our schedules make it harder and harder to refuse our children's demands.

There are plenty of completely legitimate reasons why we

have come to rely on technology more to keep our children occupied. The changes in our family structure, neighborhoods, work lives, and educational system have all pushed us in this direction. We parents are not blameless for the number of hours our children are on screens, but we are also not living in a vacuum. We are living in a world where phones and tablets and laptops are ubiquitous and we rarely pause to think about the effects of them.

Very few parents look at their children and their families and think, "You know what would make my children happier and healthier? You know what would make my family's life calmer, warmer, and more fulfilling? More screen time."

## CHAPTER 2

# Babies Aren't Meant to Be Einsteins

■ ■ ■ ■

THERE IS ONE AREA where parents believe that screen time could be beneficial—early childhood education. The notion that not giving your kids—even very young ones—the most advanced technology puts them at a disadvantage came up again and again throughout my interviews with parents. And it's easy to understand how companies manipulate even the most educated mothers and fathers into believing this—especially when you consider how many other things they have been manipulated into believing.

"We see it as an acknowledgment by the leading baby video company that baby videos are not educational, and we hope other baby media companies will follow suit," Susan Linn, director of Campaign for a Commercial-Free Childhood, told the *New York Times* in 2009.[1] Her statement came after the Walt Disney Company announced it was offering refunds to anyone who had purchased a Baby Einstein video. Founded in 1997 and purchased by Disney in 2001, Baby Einstein told parents that their video of brightly shaped objects with classical music playing in the background, "reinforces number recognition using simple patterns" and "introduces [children to] circles, ovals, triangles, squares and rectangles." But Baby Einstein products were not turning babies into Einsteins.

The Campaign for a Commercial-Free Childhood complained to the Federal Communications Commission about Disney's claims, threatening a class action lawsuit over what the advocacy group saw as deceptive practices. There was no evidence, it noted, to suggest that these videos offered any educational benefits, and there was evidence of potential harm for children in watching too much television at early ages. Nevertheless, a 2003 survey revealed that as many as one in three American babies between six months and two years had at least one of these videos.[2]

How did that kind of market domination occur? And how did we even get "baby media companies" to begin with?

Did a third of American parents genuinely believe that these videos—which included *Baby Einstein, Baby Mozart, Baby Galileo,* and *Baby Shakespeare*—were going to make their children smarter? Alma Schneider of Montclair, New Jersey, told the *New York Times*: "You want to make sure you're doing everything you can for your child, and you know everyone else uses 'Baby Einstein,' so you feel guilty if you don't."[3]

Geula Zamist, director of the Early Childhood Center at Congregation Agudath Israel in New Jersey, says that she recalls plenty of parents "bought into it." Though few asked for her opinion, she remembers them discussing their purchases openly. Back then, when she worked at a preschool on the Upper East Side of Manhattan, it was all the rage to have screens in the classrooms as well. It was considered "progressive." If anything, parents were trying to create what they saw as the educational atmosphere of preschool at a younger and younger age in their homes.

High-tech toys are not new. Thomas Edison invented the first talking doll in 1890—researchers were recently able to piece together a recording of its creepy voice—and they have been alternately annoying and engaging us ever since. In some ways, these toys are most tempting to offer to young children—who never seem to tire of pressing buttons and getting a voice response. But babies and toddlers may benefit from them the least.

A 2015 article in the journal *Mind, Brain, and Education* suggests that even educational electronic toys may hinder children's interactions with real people.[4] Researchers compared children who were looking at shapes on a screen and those who were looking at real objects and recorded the words of parents who were interacting with them. They concluded that "traditional toys . . . sparked higher quality conversations," which included more descriptive and useful vocabulary.

As the authors wrote in an article on the Brookings Institution website:

> These results offer just a first glimpse of differences in those old fashioned toys and the new and improved toys that seem to have a life of their own. We might have thought that these bells and whistles would enhance the educational value of the toy. Our results, however, suggest otherwise.
>
> When they're in front of a screen they turn into vegetables, staring at it slack-jawed. . . . And they align with findings from other studies suggesting that when adult-child pairs play around electronic toys, adults are less responsive to children's attentional bids than when playing with traditional toys, there is less pretense and elaboration with e-toys than with traditional toys, and that when parents read e-books rather than traditional books to their three-year-olds, their children are less likely to follow the plotline of the story.[5]

It would be surprising if these findings were not true. After all, the reason we are introducing electronics in the first place is often to lessen the burdens on ourselves. If a toy is talking to our children or making noises or flashing symbols, we feel less obliged to do anything. Even more so than with electronic toys, the way to play with a screen is instantly obvious to children. In most cases, they just have to sit on the couch and watch images on the screen in front of them. So our parental input feels pleasantly superfluous, even if for only a brief period of time.

Since the advent of *Sesame Street* in 1969, however, parents have touted the benefits, and even relied upon certain kinds, of children's television not only to entertain their children but to educate them. And some research supports this point of view.

In a paper published in 2015 by the National Bureau of Economic Research, economists Melissa Kearney of the University of Maryland and Phillip Levine of Wellesley released results from a large longitudinal study on *Sesame Street*. Because *Sesame Street* was available in some areas before others in the 1960s (thanks to the vagaries of early TV broadcasting, not socioeconomic factors), the authors used census data to compare the outcomes of kids who were able to watch it with those who couldn't:

> We relate this geographic variation to outcomes in Census data including grade-for-age status in 1980, educational attainment in 1990, and labor market outcomes in 2000. The results indicate that *Sesame Street* accomplished its goal of improving school readiness; preschool-aged children in areas with better reception when it was introduced were more likely to advance through school as appropriate for their age.[6]

The authors found that "this effect is particularly pronounced for boys and non-Hispanic, black children, as well as children living in economically disadvantaged areas."[7]

In an interview following the release of this report, Levine told the *Atlantic* that *Sesame Street* was "the largest and least-costly [early childhood] intervention that's ever been implemented" in the United States.[8] Indeed, while Head Start now costs about $7,600 annually per child, according to Kearney and Levine, the annual per-child cost of *Sesame Street* (in today's dollars) is just $5. Of course, since the most recent large-scale examination of Head Start found almost no discernible effects, the bar has been set pretty low.

The National Bureau of Economic Research paper certainly was the most positive in addressing the educational benefits of children's programming. However, a variety of studies have looked at the question of whether children are learning anything from so-called educational shows. As soon as 1971, a few years after *Sesame Street* went on the air, a study conducted by the Russell Sage Foundation questioned some of the early excitement about the show's effects.

First, it found that at least some of the gains were largely among kids who received "encouragement to view."[9] That is, people visited and called the kids' families, impressing on them the importance of watching *Sesame Street*. Among the general audience of *Sesame Street*, there were some learning gains, but "only one test (Letters) reached conventional statistical criteria of educational significance." On the other hand, "encouragement-and-viewing decreased the amount that disadvantaged parents reported reading to their children."[10] It's possible that parents who received encouragement to view were actually viewing the show with the kids and interacting with them while it was on. That, in and of itself, can influence the ways in which kids absorb information.

The effects of *Sesame Street* were mixed, but the authors found something else interesting. "We have been struck," they write, "by the frequency with which parents were skeptical about our finding that six-months' viewing of *Sesame Street* led to little cognitive gain." One reason for that, they speculate, is that parents "may have been thrilled that their child learned something from the program and might have generalized from the learning of some items to the learning of more significant ones." Or it's possible that *Sesame Street* has generated such favorable press that parents assume their children are learning. But most interestingly for our purposes, "viewers might have learned some items from the program which, at their stage of development they would have learned from their environment anyway."[11]

Indeed, the question for parents is not whether a particular show can teach children something. It's whether they wouldn't learn those ideas if the television were off. It's particularly concerning that parents who were encouraged to have their children view *Sesame Street* gave up time reading with their children in order to give them more time in front of the television.

*Sesame Street* is certainly better than nothing—that is, it's better than no one talking or reading to a child. If the choice is between having a child watch *Sesame Street* or soap operas, *Sesame Street* is preferable. If there is no adult who is going to interact with the child, *Sesame Street* is preferable. But whether *Sesame Street* is preferable to a child simply listening to his or her family's conversation is questionable.

The parents I interviewed had a variety of criteria they used for picking shows for their children. *SpongeBob Square-Pants* came up quite a bit in my interviews. The wildly popular show ran for nine seasons, and it seems to have had enduring appeal for a variety of age groups. It is a show that can put my nine-year-old, seven-year-old, and four-year-old into a coma-like state almost instantly.

Some parents suspected the show was bad for their kids,

but most acknowledged that the show's noise, strange images, and nonsensical plots just drove adults crazy. Joanne remembers her husband one day came home with some videos he had rented, and *SpongeBob* was among them. "I put it in and sat there with my daughter 20 minutes. It was so obnoxious. She still talks about it, but we never watch it. I preferred more low-key, less crazy."

Josh, a father of three in Pittsburgh, tells me, "My big concern from the beginning is if I show my kids fast moving images, they will be bored in school." His children don't watch cartoons, but he will let them watch soccer. "All they will see is a big green field."

A number of parents mentioned *Caillou* and *Thomas the Tank Engine* as the kind of slow-moving programs that they think are more appropriate and sometimes more educational. And there is no reason for parents to doubt their instincts on this. If watching these shows gives you a headache—if all the rapid movement of characters and loud noises emanating from the television is too much for you—chances are it's not great for your child either. You don't need a scientific study on *SpongeBob* to ban it from your home.

But the shows that parents find most palatable are not necessarily educational. As Malcolm Gladwell recounts in his book *The Tipping Point*, studies showed the kids who watched *Blue's Clues* learned more than those who watched *Sesame Street*.[12] The former was repetitive, had long pauses, and had a limited cast of characters. All of that made it easier for kids to follow. But it was of significantly less entertainment value to adults. *Sesame Street*, meanwhile, continued to grow its adult audience with the presence of popular actors, musicians, and even politicians—many of whom young kids would never recognize. *Sesame Street* is still on the air; *Blue's Clues* is not.

It is worth noting, though, that one of the more popular

recent additions to public television's offerings for kids has been *Daniel Tiger's Neighborhood.* The show, a spin-off of *Mr. Roger's Neighborhood,* is actually much closer to *Blue's Clues* than *Sesame Street.* Kids are taught a one-line song about sharing or what to do when you're angry or using the bathroom, and it is repeated throughout the episode in different scenarios. Parents may not find these episodes particularly scintillating, but they seem to appreciate the learning that goes on.

In 2008, researchers at the University of Massachusetts Amherst and the University of California Riverside published an article in the *Future of Children,* a collaboration of Princeton University and the Brookings Institution. They found:

> When studies control for important confounding variables such as income and parent education, they often fail to find significant linear relations between television viewing and subsequent achievement. In fact, the association appears to be curvilinear, with achievement increasing to a peak at low levels of television viewing (one to two hours a day), and then declining with heavier viewing.[13]

In general, they observed that "educational programs are positively associated with overall measures of achievement and with potentially long-lasting effects, while purely entertainment content, particularly violent content, is negatively associated with academic achievement."[14] However, it's difficult to distinguish correlation from causation, since many of the homes that restrict television use are also the ones that encourage viewing of educational programs, and those that allow heavy television viewing may also allow fare that's inappropriate for younger viewers.

A 2004 article in *Pediatrics* by Dimitri A. Christakis of Seattle Children's Hospital found that "early exposure to television was associated with subsequent attentional problems."[15] Even when controlling for socioeconomic status, gestational age, and other factors, the authors discovered that an increase of one standard deviation in the number of hours of television watched at age one "is associated with a 28 percent increase in the probability of having attentional problems at age 7." Every additional hour of TV consumption increased a child's odds of having attention problems by about 10 percent. Kids who watched three hours a day were 30 percent more likely to have attention trouble than those who watched none.[16]

In the wake of the study, one physician offered this commentary, also in *Pediatrics*:

> Approximately 3 decades ago, teachers of young children at all socioeconomic levels began to report troubling changes in their students, mainly centering on decreasing abilities to listen, pay attention, and engage in independent problem solving. Frequently, the teachers blamed the advent of fast-paced, attention-getting children's programming for this trend. Now that the trend is viewed nationally as an "epidemic" of ADHD [attention deficit hyperactivity disorder], perhaps it is indeed time to ask the research questions so ably initiated by Christakis et al. and to consider that pediatricians may have yet one more job to do in early parent education about placing limits on screen time.[17]

In his book *The Disappearance of Childhood*, Neil Postman writes, "In truth, there is no such thing on TV as children's programming. Everything is for everybody."[18] He does not mean that all content is necessarily appropriate for everyone. But, he argues, it is universally accessible. "Television offers a fairly primitive but irresistible alternative to the linear and sequential logic of the printed word and tends to make the rigors of literate education irrelevant. There are no ABCs for pictures. In learning to interpret the meaning of images, we do not require lessons in grammar or spelling or logic or vocabulary." Postman concludes, "So far as symbolic form is concerned, *Laverne & Shirley* is as simple to grasp as *Sesame Street*; a McDonald's commercial is as simple to grasp as a Xerox commercial."[19] This is why, even before the advent of Netflix and round-the-clock children's cartoon networks, millions of kids were glued to the television in the evenings— when nothing "appropriate" was on. There is something about all television programs that will attract a young child's attention.

Danielle, a mother of four children under the age of eight, says, "My kids are really TV obsessed. If we're anywhere and there's a TV on, their tongues are out and they're staying." When they go visit their cousins, where the television is on consistently in the background, Danielle has to ask her sister-in-law to turn it off so her children will do other things. As adults, we have grown used to the idea that there are multiple things competing for our attention and we have to tune out some things in order to concentrate on others. It's debatable how well we do this, but young kids don't seem to do it well at all.

There is a growing body of research on how multitasking with electronics tends to distract students from schoolwork and decrease the amount of information they are able to absorb (a subject to which we will return to in a later chapter), but for most parents of young kids, this problem is exceedingly obvious. Just try to get a toddler's attention to do anything while they have an iPad in front of them or there is a television on—no matter what program is running.

Just because a child really seems into a show is not necessarily a sign that the child is learning anything from it. Rather, it is likely that the show is distracting the child in a way that human voices or inanimate objects are not.

. . . .

In the introduction to the twenty-fifth anniversary edition of his book *The Hurried Child*, psychologist David Elkind notes that the "most significant transformation in children's lives [since his book was published in 1981] has to do with the new attention to stimulating infants and young children. Infancy and early childhood are now the focus of hurrying."[20] Providing them with videos and learning products at such a young age is a way of pushing them into later childhood and even adulthood much faster than is necessary or desirable. If everyone else is doing it, though, we don't want our children to be left behind.

It is only natural that companies trying to make money would take advantage of parents' confusion and capacity for guilt to sell us absurd products. In 2015, a Spanish outfit called Babypod introduced a "vaginal speaker." "Babies learn to speak in response to sound stimuli, especially melodic sound. Babypod is a device that stimulates before birth through music. With Babypod, babies learn to vocalise from the womb," read the blurb on the company's website.[21] The fact that people actually purchased this product may be a sign of too much disposable income. Elkind provides some much-needed perspective about these products:

> The promoters of these products play on our paren-
> tal guilt and anxiety about our children's ability to

compete in an increasingly technological and global economy. These concerns are understandable, but they are also a little misguided. What infants need most, and what will give them the best foundation for whatever world they are going to live in, is not provided by any computer program. What they need most is a healthy sense that the world is a safe place, that their needs will be met, and that they will be cared for and protected by the grown-ups in their world.[22]

Many parents presumably saw through the silliness of Baby Einstein videos. They didn't really think these random objects on a screen accompanied by soothing music were going to turn their child into Harvard material. Baby Einstein videos were simply a way of keeping a baby occupied for a few minutes. It didn't work for every child, but plenty of nine-month-olds were transfixed.

There is nothing wrong with the desire to keep our kids occupied. But what does it mean to occupy a child? And is technology the only or best way to accomplish this?

The feeling of being responsible for another human being is something that fills many of us with fear and confusion. A former colleague of mine, a staunch libertarian, once recounted the story of the birth of her first child. After a couple of uneventful days in the hospital, the nurse told her it was time to go home with her newborn daughter. My colleague, who generally wanted the government to stop interfering in any aspect of her life, suddenly felt a surge of terror and surprise. "Wait, you're going to let me take this thing home? I have no idea what I'm doing. Shouldn't there be a test or something?"

Our parents and grandparents may not have experienced similar fears because intergenerational households were more common. These days we spend less time around babies because of our smaller families. The fact that childbearing is a choice rather than an expectation also makes it seem like a greater responsibility. If you have decided after more than a decade of adulthood to have a baby, you are surely going to be held accountable for any failure to bring it up right.

Which is actually pretty reasonable. But instead of parents taking this pressure as a cue to watch their children and think hard about the possible perverse effects of putting them in front of baby videos instead of, say, getting out the pots and pans and letting them bang away, it has only increased the herd mentality and hastened the stampede for more baby media.

The fear that we will do something wrong—something that will put our kids at a disadvantage physically, emotionally, or intellectually—actually begins long before the birth of the child. In recent decades, we have been able to learn more and more about what goes on in the womb. We have come to understand not just that pregnant mothers shouldn't smoke or drink or use drugs because of the danger of birth defects. Future parents walk around showing off sonogram pictures to perfect strangers. We can see babies reacting to different stimuli on highly detailed screens. Doctors can now perform prenatal surgeries, fixing health problems in fetuses even before they are fully developed. In many respects, this new knowledge has been deeply beneficial for babies and the mothers who want them to live long healthy lives.

But our window into the womb has also made us a little bit crazy. Just consider the shelves of books on advice about pregnancy. Or the list of foods that you should not eat. Or the activities you should not partake in. Pregnant women can be in a constant state of anxiety over all of the advice and prohibitions they hear from doctors, friends, and some random woman watching them drink a glass of wine in a restaurant. The only time in my life someone has given me a book and then advised me *not to read all of it* was when a nurse gave me a copy of *What to Expect When You're Expecting*. It is filled with hundreds and hundreds of pages of everything that can go wrong in the nine months of pregnancy.

In 2013, Fisher Price released (just in time for the holidays) the "Newborn-to-Toddler Apptivity Seat for iPad." It's a baby seat with a plastic case designed to hold an iPad right in front of a baby's eyes. As the product description explains: "Lock your iPad device inside the case to protect from dribbles and drool. Play and learning are at baby's fingertips." The Apptivity seat will probably provide hours of entertainment for your child, but is that what he or she needs?

A study that year by Common Sense Media found that children under the age of one spend at least an hour in front of a television or mobile device per day, and the average two- to four-year-old spends about two hours a day in front of screens.[23] Children this age are only awake for ten to twelve hours a day—so that screen time amounts to about a fifth or sixth of their waking hours. The question is what would they do if they didn't have the screen in front of them.

Frankly, infants would probably cry for some of the time. But they also might stare at the ceiling for a while or play with their toes. As babies get older, they'd play with some blocks or chew on a teething toy or throw a stuffed animal over the side of a playpen. They might babble or try out new words. But the fact that they might be upset or bored for a few minutes leaves today's parents unsettled. Once we put the baby into the vibrating seat or the swing, we are trying to get something done—laundry, dishes, emails for work—and even if the baby is not screaming, each little whine is like a timer ticking down. You have one minute left before a full-on tantrum.

But when child psychologist David Elkind writes that children should grow up with a sense that the world is safe and that they will be protected, he doesn't mean that children need to have an adult or technological substitute in front of them for every waking hour or that they should never be uncomfortable and never whine.

## Tips for Cutting Back

Children are not adults. They do not like to sit still for long periods of time. If the only way you can get them to do so is with a device, ask if the children really need to be there. Whether it's a fancy restaurant or their brother's three-hour swim meet, maybe that's not where they belong.

Soon after I had my oldest daughter and I started spending time with other new moms, I heard mothers mention to me that they didn't have time to take a shower during the day. It was phrased as a kind of confession. "I forgot to brush my teeth." "I put my shirt on inside out." "I ate mashed carrots and Cheerios for lunch today."

The first few months with a newborn are filled with chaos and sleep deprivation. You may realize that you don't have any grown-up food in the house or that you forgot an important meeting. But for me, anyway, the shower was always a priority. When discussing this topic with other new moms, I learned that the mothers who did take showers often took the baby in the car seat and parked it on the bathroom floor while they bathed.

That had never occurred to me. I was not a mother who prioritized "me time," the way the self-help books advise. Indeed, for the first ten months after my oldest daughter was born, my husband was writing a book during the evenings and weekends, so me time was not really an option. But I never thought of showers as optional. When they were babies, I left my kids in their cribs while I took a shower. If the cribs were safe enough for them to sleep in for hours at a time, why not use them for a few minutes at other times of the day? Sometimes I made it into the shower while they were sleeping, but if I didn't, so what? What did single mothers do? Or people who didn't have a babysitter? What would my own mother have done? Or my grandmother?

No mother likes to hear her baby cry. According to a 2012 article in the *Journal of Neuroscience*, a baby crying ranked as one of the top ten most annoying sounds in the world.[23] But I'm only being somewhat flip when I say that the joy of being in the shower is that you can't actually hear them cry.

When they were big enough to get out of the crib, I used a gate to lock them in their rooms. Those rooms were childproofed—no live wires, but no padded walls either. If they wanted to yell for the six minutes I was out of sight, they were welcome to it. But even at a young age, they learned quickly that those were minutes when they'd have to entertain themselves.

When I speak with other parents and educators, they are quick to warn me that a lot of kids are unwilling or unable to entertain themselves for long periods of time. And we certainly don't want to get into the habit of assuming infants or toddlers should be left alone—even in a safe environment—for more than a few minutes. God knows, I'd be arrested for running into the dry cleaner while a baby was safely buckled in a car seat. But if the standard we set for ourselves is that a child must be completely satisfied and engaged by an adult from morning until the night, we have made our jobs as parents impossible. There are few adults who have the patience or energy for this. The alternative, we come to believe, is to hire a babysitter or, more conveniently and cheaply, use a screen.

Emily Friere, mother of a nine-month-old, wrote a piece for the *Federalist* about how she is trying to restrict her daughter's screen time. She admired actor Damien Lewis for enforcing no screen time during the week with his children. But then she dismissed Lewis and his wife as having an unfair advantage. "When I'm tired I sometimes wish there was a way to get her to sit quietly for just 20 minutes while I rest or accomplish a few tasks. [They] can hand their kids to a nanny at that point. For many other parents, putting in a DVD is the answer."[24]

Of course, wealthy celebrities will always have an advantage when it comes to childcare. But some pundits and scholars have recently suggested that discouraging mothers from putting their kids in front of a screen for hours a day is sexist. Writing on *JSTOR Daily*, Alexandra Samuel noted, "When we worry that parents are shirking their duties by relying on an electronic babysitter, we're really worrying that mothers are putting their own needs alongside, or even ahead of, their kids' needs. . . . Our anxiety about making mothers' work easier is rooted in our profound reservations about liberating women from the demands of the home."[25]

As someone who both thinks mothers of young children should shower daily and believes we should restrict kids' screen time, I think Samuel is wrong. Concerns that children are overly dependent on technology for their entertainment are not actually part of some kind of conspiracy to keep women down. Somehow mothers (even single ones) managed to run errands and do chores and even hold down jobs before the invention of iPads.

There are all sorts of reasons why older children want technology, as we will see in the chapters that follow. They want to keep in touch with their friends. They like to compete at video games. They like making YouTube videos of themselves. But for children between infancy and three years old, the impetus for the increase in screen time is coming from parents, not children. Why do we think our babies and toddlers—just learning how to navigate the world—should have access to television (educational or otherwise) or tablets?

Plenty of conscientious parents give kids screens long before their pediatricians think it's a good idea. They do it because the messages of our culture about parenting—from doctors and teachers to product advertisements and parenting handbooks—tell us that our kids need to be occupied, engaged, and satisfied at all times.

We have come to believe that babies need to be distracted and that in order for us to get anything done they must be completely engrossed—or at least sleeping. If we are not feeding them or changing them or bathing them or taking them to mommy and me classes, they should be doing *something*. They have to be stimulated. Indeed, if they're not, they're probably falling behind. Perhaps these goals are possible to accomplish with only one child, but even this style of parenting is pretty exhausting. With two children, it's nearly impossible.

Therefore, in order to decrease the amount of technology we give our kids, we need to first let ourselves off the hook. Only once we set reasonable standards for our children's gratification will we be able to set reasonable goals for how to parent with technology.

## CHAPTER 3

# Are You Preparing Your Child for School or Las Vegas?

■ ■ ■ ■

IF WE GIVE TECHNOLOGY to children between infancy and age three in order to distract them, we offer it to children between four and eight in order to promote early learning and school readiness. In spring 2016, I ran a small survey to find out how parents were using technology with their kids.[1] Half of parents with children between the ages of zero and six said they were using technology to prepare their kids for school. And 46 percent of parents with kids ages seven to twelve said the same thing.

"We downloaded games that we felt were educational," says Lisa, a mother of three in suburban New Jersey. Lisa, who works at a large bank in New York, says that she did not approve of many of the iPad activities available, referring to them as "mind rot." But when her oldest was four, she said, "we used a lot of spelling games, word games, and math games." She read the reviews of the apps on the iTunes store before purchasing them to make sure they were "educational."

Many of the parents I spoke to are like Lisa—diligent when it comes to investigating the games they let their kids play. Some give their kids devices at home. Others let kids play on the computers at the library. A trip to any children's library section will reveal a line of kids waiting to use the screens. Parents feel certain that any game on the library computer will be educational in some way. No one wants to hold a child back.

Lowell Monke, a professor of education at Wittenberg

University, has written extensively on the relationship between technology and learning. Parents, he tells me, are "so proud of how their kids can handle this incredibly complicated stuff and so worried their kids will fall behind because that's what the future is all about." They worry that if their kids don't start using technology early, "they will be left out of it." Even if parents worry about screen time, he says, they have a "religious reverence for technology. We fear it, but in the long run we believe in it." Unfortunately, we may be waiting until the Messiah comes for the evidence that technology is helping our kids educationally.

Computers did not start out in the hands of children. They were machines meant to improve the work of grown-ups—to make us faster and more efficient at our jobs and in managing our personal affairs. (It's good to remember that efficiency is not a goal we have for our children's development.) But over time, the technology trickled down. Adult consumers began to use computers more in their homes—still for tasks that were obligatory, from personal finance to writing letters.

Most kids in the 1980s, for instance, had little interest in personal computers. There were other screens that were keeping them occupied at the time. In 1984, Nintendo released an entertainment system for the home. Children's attention was held for hours on end by the new video game systems that could be hooked up to the family television. From *Donkey Kong* to *The Legend of Zelda* to *Mario Bros.*, children were enthralled by the games they could experience in their living rooms instead of waiting for someone to drive them to the arcade.

At schools, meanwhile, if children had any access to computers, it was to Radio Shack's Tandy models and some early Macintoshes. Students did little besides learn to type codes that would get computers to spit words or line drawings back to them. There was no competition with video games. But slowly things began to shift. Computer technology gained more potential for entertainment as well as education.

In her book *Engineering Play: A Cultural History of Children's Software*, Mizuko Ito explains: "When PCs [personal computers] became a viable consumer technology, software developers and educators began developing new genres of software and public scripts about computational media and learning. They argued that the new interactive media held out the potential to challenge the dominance of 'passive' forms of media that were exemplified by the television." In other words, Ito writes, "the computer was defined as a 'good screen' that was contrasted to the 'bad screen' of the television."[2]

Many parents began to see in computers the opportunity to give their children the academic skills they needed in a more fun way. While my friends were playing *Pac-Man*, my sister and I were offered *Where in the World Is Carmen San Diego?* It was billed as a kind of mystery game players had to solve, but in order to arrive at the correct answer, at some point you had to look up places or famous people in an encyclopedia that came with the software. (This was before Google, so it was an actual encyclopedia.) If you think about it, this was a strange activity to give to young children. Under what circumstances would our parents have suggested in our spare time that we look up items in an encyclopedia? And under what circumstances would we have said yes? But somehow the sound the computer made when we clicked the right answer made it seem like this was a good game.

Similarly, while most mothers and fathers would never make their four-year-old practice flash cards at the kitchen table, they happily hand the child an iPad with *Math Bingo* or a spelling game. Parents assume that as long as the child is enjoying the experience of pressing the button and hearing the resulting joyful noise or watching the animated fireworks when getting something right, then the software itself must be good for the child.

While parents have generally seen television, even educational television, as a kind of necessary indulgence—something to keep the kids busy—educational software is something different.

And it's easy to understand why. When my son was four, someone recommended a game called *Map It*. Within a couple of weeks of putting it on our iPad, my son was able to identify the location of all 50 states on a blank map—something I was required to do in fourth grade and am not sure I could do successfully right now. It was a neat party trick, and he was happy to hear his grandparents applaud his new skill. Obviously, we would not have given him an atlas and instructed him to memorize U.S. geography. But the funny sounds and the googly eyes on the shapes of the states made it fun. Surely this cannot be put in the same category as watching television, even educational television.

But are computers and tablets better for kids than TV? There is some degree to which it matters what kids are doing with each. Can you compare a child watching a documentary about whales with a child playing tennis on the Wii or a child watching a soccer game with one playing *Minecraft* on an iPad? Playing with Webkinz on a computer or seeing *Super Why!* on Netflix? There is a vast universe of television programming and computer software out there, and one can always try to make the case for the value of some particular program on either screen.

Dimitri Christakis, a researcher from Seattle Children's Hospital, suggests that there is reason to suspect apps on a tablet are better for kids than television because they can say "I did it" with the former but not the latter. In a TED talk he gave in 2015, Christakis describes the way even babies like to drop things from a high chair and watch an adult pick them up and put them back. "They love that they make something happen in the real world. High quality apps [in which kids can make things happen] are very different from passive media."[3]

But he also suggests that the evidence in this area is still thin. While he and others have started to do research on the way kids use touchscreen technology, he warned, "Science cannot keep up with the pace of technological advances."[4] When it comes to our kids, we are in the midst of a "large uncontrolled experiment."

Let's just pause for a minute to acknowledge that when it comes to anything else besides technology, most parents would be hesitant to throw their kids into a large uncontrolled experiment. Just imagine: "Here's some food we haven't tested—no idea if it's healthy or harmful. See if the kids like it." "Here's some new pajamas that may or may not be flame retardant—still experimenting. Wanna try them out?" "Here's a car with an airbag that may or may not deploy. We're still working out the kinks." It's unlikely any of these tests would tempt parents. But with technology, they want to be on the cutting edge.

Christakis and his team have looked at the way attention is affected by television (as we discussed in the previous chapter), and they have concluded that the effects in entertainment (as opposed to educational) television can have a real impact on kids' attention spans later on. But comparing the effects of playing on a computer or a tablet with watching television have not advanced much yet. This is in part because the technology keeps changing and in part because it is hard to make apples-to-apples comparisons.

Where are the studies, for instance, on whether watching *Dora the Explorer* on a television is better than playing a Dora game on a computer? In both cases, kids will hear Dora giving directions in English and Spanish. On television, she will ask them to repeat after her. They may or may not comply. On the computer, kids are asked to press a button to signify that they understand what she's saying. In the case of the latter, we assume that children clicking on a particular part of the screen implies that they have made a real effort to understand Dora, whereas if they are just lying back on the couch not pressing buttons, they may be only half-listening. Does the use of "agency" mean that kids are going to learn more?

These assumptions both overestimate the extent to which kids are really paying attention to the content of educational software and underestimate how much they're paying attention to television. Kids certainly do take in information from television shows (otherwise, as others have pointed out, why would advertisers spend billions of dollars a year on television commercials?). And many children couldn't care less about whether they are entering the correct answers on their PBS Kids app. They just want to press the colorful buttons over and over. They get the "I did it" feeling either way.

Indeed, there is nothing like buttons, electronic or otherwise, to make a young child happy. My children still fight over who gets to press buttons in elevators and we live in the greater New York area where it's hardly a unique experience.

There is some deep satisfaction that children get out of pressing circles that light up. Even before touchscreen technology, kids enjoyed clicking on computer icons or Speak & Spell or buttons on a tape deck. Maybe it's what Christakis says—that they enjoy the ability to affect outcomes whether it's on the screen or in the real world—but I think there's something else at work here as well.

It's the same kind of joy that adults get from playing *Candy Crush* on their phones. *Candy Crush*, along with *Candy Crush*

*Soda Saga*, clocks in ninety-two million users daily. That's a lot of buttons being pressed—and no adult would seriously argue that they are learning anything from these games. What makes us unable to stop pressing these buttons— even while we are supposed to be doing something else? Researchers say that by limiting the amount of time a user can be on *Candy Crush*, game designers leave users always wanting more. Others note that *Candy Crush* is mostly a game of chance but it leaves users feeling as if they have some small amount of control over the outcomes. This too seems to make players less likely to stop.

When I talked to Julia Kim—a college classmate of mine who has worked on technology for both the private sector and the federal government—about kids and technology, she suggested I consider the research on slot machines. The 2012 book *Addiction by Design: Machine Gambling in Las Vegas* is one of the most disturbing accounts of modern life in America you would want to read, and it also offers tremendous insight into the ways people of all ages use technology and the reasons we can't seem to stop.

Interviewing a woman named Mollie at the MGM Grand in Las Vegas, author Natasha Dow Schüll, a professor at the Massachusetts Institute of Technology (MIT), asks if she was hoping for a big win. In response, Mollie gives a short laugh and a dismissive wave of her hand. "In the beginning, there was excitement about winning," she says, "but the more I gambled, the wiser I got about my chances. Wiser but also weaker, less able to stop. Today when I win—and I do win from time to time—I just put it back in the machines. The thing people never understand is that *I'm not playing to win*."[5]

So why *does* Mollie play? "To keep playing—to stay in that machine zone where nothing else matters." What is the machine zone? Mollie tries to explain: "It's like being in the eye of a storm, is how I'd describe it. Your vision is clear on the machine in front of you but the whole world is spinning around you, and you can't really hear anything. You aren't really there—you're with the machine and that's all you're with."[6]

It is easy to think that Mollie's description of her experience with machine gambling is not relevant to the way other adults play *Candy Crush* or kids play *Subway Surfer* or even *Map It*, but the truth is more complicated. The gamblers that Schüll interviews say repeatedly that winning is not really the point, even that money is not really the point. It's being in this "zone."

The adults Schüll speaks to are an extreme case, to be sure. They are so engaged in the games they're playing they lose track of time. Some forget to go to the bathroom. If you've ever potty-trained a child, you know that screen time is your enemy. It's so easy for kids at that stage to lose awareness of themselves when they are watching television or playing on a tablet. The trance-like state they enter during screen time is exactly the opposite of what's required to, as Grover says on *Elmo's Potty Time* video, "listen to your body." When you're playing a game or watching a show, there's no natural stopping point. The screen activity keeps on going and so you feel you must keep going with it.

Schüll describes not only how screen games work to shut out the world but how they encourage players to take measures to shut it out even more. According to the people who design casino floors, players gravitate toward "insulated enclaves," inside "small alcoves, recesses and corners," "sheltered in nooks and crannies." As one player told Schüll, "I want to be in my own little cave."[7] I was startled by this image, particularly because of the way I see my kids and others using tablets—curling up in corners, getting as far away from others as possible. My oldest daughter took to watching the iPad while entirely under a blanket as if she had retreated into her own little tent.

Before I take the analogy too far, I should say that plenty of kids like to curl up with a good book too. But as we will explore later, the trance-like state that kids seem to enter with technology seems qualitatively different from the one they enter with an engrossing novel.

Nonetheless, it is interesting that adults who are using these slot machines actually seem to be reverting to more child-like ways. Just like kids enjoy creating little forts in which to protect themselves from the outside world, adults on casino floors seem to want "sanctuaries of play." One explained, "I'd gravitate toward corners, where it felt safe and I could get into my zone."

We can learn a lot about casino gamblers' behavior because there are security cameras on them all the time. Those cameras have captured people so much in the zone that they don't even notice when a customer sitting next to them actually collapses from a heart attack and an entire emergency team comes to respond.

So what does it mean to get into the zone? What people are describing is something akin to flow—a concept discussed in the introduction. Mihaly Csikszentmihalyi acknowledges that any flow activity is "potentially addictive,"[8] though he suggests that whether it is or not has more to do with the propensities of a particular person rather than the aspects of a particular activity. That may be true, but it does seem that game designers have every incentive to make them more addictive, not less. Whether it's online gambling or *Candy Crush* or *Math Bingo*, there are many people who will just want to keep playing—not to win money, not to win at all, but just to stay in the zone.

Schüll argues that both video games and machine gambling have to do with "the affective equilibration of the zone." By this she means that both gamblers and game users "most readily enter the zone at the point where their own actions become indistinguishable from the functioning of the machines." The gamblers describe how what they want to happen and what happens seems to occur at the exact same time. "My eyes feel like they're lining up the bars on the screen—I see them turning, and then stop, *like they're under my influence.*"[9]

Maybe this sounds creepy, but Schüll finds direct parallels between this and the experience that young children seem to enjoy with their mothers—mothers adapting to their babies needs almost immediately, realizing when they're hungry, sensing when they're about to wake up, understanding when they need to be held. Before a child can even think to want something, a mother is there to provide it. But over time, the gap between a child's desire and a parent's response lengthens. And children, thankfully, adapt to this change, learning to wait longer for a response to their needs and actions.

But some children do not adapt. Autistic children, when they are distressed, continue to prefer what Schüll calls "object-based interactions that allow close-to-perfect stimulus response contingencies, such as bouncing a ball or pressing a button." The same moment you press a button, it makes a noise or it lights up.[10]

A lot of researchers have looked into the question of why autistic children seem so interested in and at ease with technology. While the scholars who study autism often have different understandings of it, many of them seem to agree that children "on the spectrum" like the predictability of technology. Every time you press a button there are a limited number of possible effects. And all of them are immediate.

Mark Riedl, a professor of computing at Georgia Tech who has been working on developing technology to help autistic children learn how to navigate social situations, notes, "This is a population that relates to tech because it's safe and secure. You can learn rules of a computer program and predict what will happen."

For autistic kids who may have trouble navigating what they are supposed to do—for instance, when they walk into a movie theater or a restaurant—the games are supposed to get as close as possible to real life. As Riedl explains, it is sort of like a "choose-your-own-adventure" game.

But as Riedl and others tell me, it's very hard to get kids to apply what they've learned in a computer game to a real-life setting. For the population he is dealing with, he says he is "worried about the gamification aspects" of what many people in this field are developing. "Things that are too much like games may divert your attention from what's going on." It may seem as if the more fun you can make something, the more kids will be likely to use it and the more they will learn. But Riedl argues this is not always the case.

Agata Rozga, a developmental psychologist and a colleague of Riedl's at Georgia Tech, believes that rather than just giving autistic kids buttons to press in a game, we have to harness their attraction to technology to get them to engage with other kids. Giving kids tasks they have to do *with someone else* on the computer might accomplish this.

She notes that even for kids who aren't on the spectrum, playing with other kids can be more difficult than playing with a screen. "Why do we like watching television?" she asks. "It's this very easy, passive way to spend time. You don't have to do anything." But even with many computer games there is an ease in playing simply because they are predictable.

Interacting with other people is something entirely different. "To play is to be generative. It's challenging to play with other kids. You have to be negotiating and navigating, coordinating with another person," says Rozga. In order to play with another child or an adult, there has to be give and take. By contrast, "in front of a game, you have full control. As long as the iPad is charged, you're good to go."

Rozga is not suggesting that nonautistic children always prefer a screen to playing with a friend. Indeed, as they get older, it is more likely they'd prefer a friend. For some children, though, the fast response of the game—the seeming synchronization of their desires and the machine's actions—can put them "in the zone" and actually have the effect of rendering them "functionally autistic," as tech researcher William Huber writes on the website *Ludonauts*.[11]

Though they may not like to admit it, parents know what it means when researchers talk about games putting their kids in the zone. They know because the zone is not where they want their kids to be. They want their kids to be aware of their surroundings, to respond when people are talking to them, to be able to pause a game without having to be dragged away from it. They don't want their kids to look like they are experiencing slot machines in Vegas.

Researchers who believe that video games can be good for children at young ages increasingly argue that "sugarcoating" games in which players get rewarded for an otherwise boring task is not the best way to use technology for learning. Those games that most resemble electronic slot machines or *Pac-Man* or *Two Dots* don't seem to encourage much creative thinking or much thinking at all. In many of these games, players never take their fingers more than a fraction of an inch away from the controller.

But in games like *Civilization* or *Minecraft* or *SimCity*, Ito remarks, "the educational content is integrally related to the game-play experience and simulation, and . . . students are actively engaged in solving problems."[12] She says the new conversation about educational video games is "less focused on games as a platform to deliver educational content and more on how game play can support a wide range of learning outcomes, both social and cognitive."[13]

Still, there are obvious limits even to what these games can teach kids. What the research on autistic kids tells us is that it is hard to translate the lessons we learn on screen into our everyday lives. *Math Bingo* will probably teach your child arithmetic that can be used in a classroom setting. But games that try to teach kids social interactions have a much higher threshold to cross. The world of people is unpredictable. The world of computers is not.

Riedl, who has a two-year-old son, believes that parents and researchers have to ask: "How do you integrate tech into people's lives in ways that doesn't cause further disruption? If we shift people on to more tech and out of society, are we causing other problems?" With kids, in particular, he worries that "if it's all time spent on screen that means it's time not spent on other things."

At an age where kids are supposed to be learning more about the world around them—both in their physical environment and in their interactions with other people—technology can seem to provide more information, but often it detracts from time spent on other things.

. . . .

"Will you prepare my child for kindergarten?" That's the question one preschool director in the New York suburbs says

she gets more than any other. "No," she tells them. "We prepare kids for life." Which sounds like a pretty cheeky answer
except when you consider that what these parents want is
to incorporate more academics into preschool. And this preschool director doesn't think that's such a great idea.

In a 2016 *Atlantic* article called "The New Preschool Is
Crushing Kids," Yale researcher Erika Christakis notes,
"Much greater portions of the day are now spent on what's
called 'seat work' (a term that probably doesn't need any
exposition) and a form of tightly scripted teaching known as
direct instruction, formerly used mainly in the older grades,
in which a teacher carefully controls the content and pacing
of what a child is supposed to learn."[14]

She argues that thanks to the pressures of No Child Left
Behind testing regimens and, more recently, the adoption
of the Common Core standards by many states, academic
pressure is being leveled at children at younger and younger
ages. Christakis writes, "Until recently, school-readiness skills
weren't high on anyone's agenda, nor was the idea that the
youngest learners might be disqualified from moving on to a
subsequent stage. But now that kindergarten serves as a gate-
keeper, not a welcome mat, to elementary school, concerns
about school preparedness kick in earlier and earlier. A child
who's supposed to read by the end of kindergarten had better
be getting ready in preschool."[15]

To say that all this pressure has simply been created by
thoughtless education policies in Washington, though, would
be an overstatement. The push to ensure that kids perform
well academically in the earliest grades was happening years
before these policies were enacted.

Take the practice of redshirting, that is, holding students
(particularly boys) back a year so that they are more capable

of sitting still and performing well academically in kindergarten. More and more parents are enrolling normal, well-functioning children in another year of preschool in order to give them a better chance of outperforming their elementary school peers. Indeed, many preschools have adapted by offering an extra "pre-K" year just for this purpose.

According to a 2000 report by the National Center for Education Statistics:

> Once it was standard practice to require kindergartners entering in September to have turned five by the following December or January; now it has become increasingly common for schools to require that children have turned five by September or October. But raising the age of eligibility has not eliminated variations in children's readiness for school, and parents and teachers have used delayed entry and retention as strategies to accommodate these variations.

According to the report, as many as 11 percent of boys were being held back in 1995. Which was, by the way, six years before No Child Left Behind was signed into law.[16]

While some parents may be pleased with the academic performance of their children as a result of keeping them back, the overall consequences of this policy have been problematic. According to a 2010 article in the *Journal of Health Economics*, "8.4 percent of children born in the month prior to their state's cutoff date for kindergarten eligibility—who typically become the youngest and most developmentally immature children within a grade—are diagnosed with ADHD, compared to 5.1 percent of children born in the month immediately afterward."[17] By suggesting that kids who enter kindergarten must be ready to do hours of seat work, we are overdiagnosing and even overmedicating children simply for being on the young end of the class.

Perhaps more than any other practice, redshirting seems to symbolize our new attitude toward preschool and the early elementary grades. The reasons behind this new pressure for kids to succeed earlier have more to do with parents and the broader culture than they do with public policy (though the two are no doubt connected).

It is worth looking at these cultural factors not only because they are clearly having some harmful effects but also because they are the impetus for giving kids technology at an early age.

■ ■ ■ ■

The pressure can be great to prepare children in preschool and early elementary school for the academic challenges that lie ahead. At the upper echelons of society, mothers and fathers are competing to get their kids into expensive preschools. But middle-class parents are also struggling to make sure that they are buying a home in the right school district (even before their kids are born). Parents read stories about how it's harder and harder to get into college, and all of that anxiety seems to have the effect of pushing children into an academic mindset earlier and earlier.

Educational technology may seem to be a vehicle for giving young children a leg up on their peers, but it may put them at a disadvantage developmentally. They are losing out on an important way to learn, to give their minds appropriate rest and to give their bodies an appropriate outlet.

And while it may seem as though our children can gain more academic skills through educational software, it is also possible that these touchscreen and button-pushing activities

are inhibiting them socially and intellectually. We are habitu-
ating them toward activities with predictable outcomes. Over
time, they may become more drawn to these activities because
they are easier than the alternative—trying to navigate new
social situations or exploring new physical environments.

CHAPTER 4

# Drop the Call—
# and the Phone While You Are at It

■ ■ ■ ■

AT A CHRISTMAS PARTY in lower Manhattan, a mother I
know was telling me why she had put off buying her
high school–age son a phone, when suddenly the boy was
standing next to us. "Mom, I'm the only ninth grader without
a phone," he complained loudly enough for his father to hear.
"Well, son," the father replied laughing, "next year you'll get
to be the only tenth grader without one."

The boy walked away crestfallen but hardly surprised.
Clearly, he was used to being the odd man out. It is probably
true that he was the last person at his prep school in New
York City to be without a phone. If their kids are going to be
walking around New York or taking subways or cabs, then
parents want them to have phones.

When do kids in the United States get their own phones?
That depends on what you mean by a phone. Plenty of parents were quick to tell me that their kids did not have a phone.
But when pressed, it turned out they had an "iTouch," which
had texting capabilities but was not a phone per se. Others
also said their kids didn't have phones, even though they had
an old phone that used to belong to Mom or Dad that could
make calls. So I wasn't entirely clear on why that didn't count.

According to the American Family Survey, parents with
children living at home say kids can "be trusted to have their
own cell phone" at the average age of 13.8. I suspect something about the wording of the question—at what age can kids

be trusted—skews the results.[1] A 2010 Kaiser Family Foundation survey found that 31 percent of eight- to ten-year-olds,
69 percent of eleven- to fourteen-year-olds, and 85 percent
of fifteen- to eighteen-year-olds owned their own phones.[2]
And that number has been steadily increasing. In 2004, for
instance, Kaiser found that among older teens, about half (56
percent) owned a cell phone.[3] And according to a 2016 study
from the marketing firm Influence Center, the average age at
which an American kid gets a phone is 10.3.[4]

In other words, kids have been getting phones at younger
and younger ages—before middle school—even if the average
parent doesn't think that kids generally should be trusted with
them until high school. The thinking seems to be: My kid can
be trusted. It's the other kids who can't.

It's similar to what parents tell their kids about driving: We
trust you. We just don't trust the other drivers. So even if we
think our own children may be responsible, we put off giving
kids a license until they are at least sixteen (or older), and
even then we add restrictions about driving at night or driving
with friends because we know a lot of kids are not going to be
responsible. Similarly, it would be naïve to think that even if
our own children are responsible with phones that their peers
will be. They're not using these devices in a vacuum.

Most of the parents I interviewed seemed to begin their
conversations about whether to get their child a cell phone
toward the end of elementary school. While it is still uncommon for kids in third grade to have a cell phone, it is not
unheard of. It certainly is the age when kids start asking for
them and when parents, at least the ones I interviewed, started
to consider them.

By the time children reach the age of eight or nine, they are
starting to construct a life for themselves that is somewhat
separate from their families. While many parents grow anx-

ious the first time their kids go off to preschool or kindergarten because they don't know what is going on during those hours, it is not until second or third grade that kids really seem to have an independent school life. This is the age when they seem to transition from having friends to having a social circle. Girls, in particular, realize how they need to act, what they need to wear, and what they need to watch in order to fit inside of a particular clique. How parents respond to this, of course, varies significantly.

Typically, kids want phones to connect with each other. And parents want phones to connect with their kids—or at least to keep track of them. Kids at this age are starting to have more freedom—depending on where they live, they may be able to walk to school or a to a friend's house or to the park. They are being dropped off at extracurricular activities, birthday parties, and play dates rather than having a parent accompany them.

When my oldest turned nine and joined a swim team, I saw the temptation immediately. I would go to pick her up from swimming, and I had other kids in the car or I was in a rush and I didn't want to have to go in and find her. I didn't know exactly how long it would take her to emerge from the locker room. Instead of getting her a phone, though, I bought her a watch. I told her what time I would meet her. And I also showed her where the front desk was at our local Y. "If you need to contact me, you go to the desk and ask the adult there to call your parents." It was not rocket science, but it required some effort. There are days that she keeps me waiting a few extra minutes and I start to get nervous, but she is at a place with other adults who know how to contact me if there is an emergency. Having to wait five extra minutes for a shower to be free is not an emergency.

But if you are genuinely concerned about emergencies, I

often wonder, why not get the kids a simple flip phone? The cell phone companies don't make it easy, but just like it's possible for the elderly to buy this less complicated option, it's certainly an option for our nine-year-olds. Still, almost no one does.

*Tips for Cutting Back*

Buy your child a watch and teach him or her how to use it. You may think that you need your kid to have a phone in order to arrange pickups and drop-offs, but you don't. Agree to meet at a time. You are not Uber. If something goes wrong, teach your child how to ask the adult present to contact you.

The concern that a child might need to contact them in case of emergency sometimes overrides any lingering doubts parents have about whether their kids are ready for the responsibility of having their own phone. Liz, a stay-at-home mother in Indianapolis, says she got her daughter a phone when she was eleven in order to communicate with her about pickups from swim practice. Her daughter also uses the phone to connect with her friends about where in the neighborhood they can meet up. And she uses Instagram to send out pictures of her artwork. Liz says that she hasn't seen any problems with her daughter's use of the phone, but she is wary. When her daughter hosts a sleepover, she is sure to collect all of the girls' phones at the beginning of evening, just in case.

Dora, who lives in the suburbs of Washington, DC, has two sons who are nine and seven. She says she might get her son a phone if he's walking to and from school by himself, but right now she doesn't know any nine-year-olds with phones. "Maybe if we lived in more hip neighborhood," she jokes. Seriously, though, Dora says that she sees a device "as a means to an end." It's possible that the end will be greater convenience. But the end might also be problematic. As Dora notes bluntly, "It's very easy to record yourself doing dumb shit and then have that available on the Internet."

One reason that Dora might not be facing this same pressure from her kids yet is that she has two boys. According to the Kaiser study, girls ages eight to eighteen typically spend ten minutes more per day talking on the phone and forty-four minutes more per day texting than boys. Girls, especially in this age range, are starting to become much more social, but with all that communication comes problems.

Lisa, the mother of a nine-year-old girl in New Jersey, says her daughter has an iTouch, which can only be used with Wi-Fi—that is, she has no data plan on it. While this probably eliminates some of the texting that her daughter can accomplish, it is very easy to access Wi-Fi in public places and at friends' houses. Even at home, though, Lisa says, she has found her daughter engrossed in texting—trying to keep up conversations with as many as ten friends at the same time.

Lisa's husband has warned their daughter, "You're going to write the wrong thing to the wrong person." Lisa says, "We try to get the idea in her head that this is not good. We've also explained to her that anything that you wouldn't say to someone in person doesn't go in a text. Once you have it out there, it can be forwarded. You can't get it back." But even with all these warnings, Lisa worries that it's just very easy for these conversations to get out of hand or even for them to be taken the wrong way. "Someone sent her a text saying, 'I got in a fight with so and so.' Before she responded, I said, 'Let's talk about how you're going to respond.'"

Still, Lisa feels that she can't restrict her daughter's texting too much because kids these days don't talk on the phone much anymore. Sometimes they use FaceTime, but mostly it's texting. It's not uncommon to hear parents say that kids these days don't talk on the phone like we used to, and so they have to accommodate texting. But there is a qualitative difference between talking on the phone and texting. For one thing, there was never a permanent record of all the dumb things we used to say on the phone to each other.

Sheila has not given her nine-year-old daughter a phone or an iTouch for exactly the reasons that Lisa elucidates. Sheila tells me, "I don't think she needs a device to complicate her communications." She's not ready for texting because she's "still learning how to behave appropriately" when she is in the same room as someone else. "Even for adults, texting has an ambiguity of tone. How often do we say: 'Oh, I didn't mean it that way!'"

Breonda also got a phone for daughter in sixth grade in order to coordinate pickups and drop-offs. It's true, she acknowledges, that people used to somehow get by without giving their kids such devices and few children were left waiting after soccer games. But in a world in which everyone else has one, it can become a problem when your child does not. If another parent decides at the last minute that she cannot pick up the kids from school or a sports practice, she will expect that all the parents will be able to contact their kids to change the plans accordingly. Indeed, it is not only for our convenience but also for the convenience of others that our children be tethered to a communication device.

The question of whether kids should be allowed to have their phones in school has roiled many administrators. They had been banned in New York City public schools in 2006, but in 2015, Mayor Bill de Blasio announced, "We have a policy right now that makes it impossible for parents to communicate with their kids. Who brought these children into the world? The parents. Who's first and foremost responsible for their safety and their well-being? The parents."[5]

Indeed, by all accounts it was parents who were pushing for this policy change, not school administrators or even kids (though they were plenty disgruntled with the former policy). Ostensibly, mothers and fathers were worried about getting in touch with their children in case of emergency. But it was also that parents were looking for the constant communication with their kids and didn't seem to mind very much if it distracted them from school.

In an article on the website *Scary Mommy* called "Why I Don't Mind When My Teenage Daughter Texts Me From School," Lisa Sadikman writes that her teenage daughter walked out in a huff one morning—the usual conflicts over getting ready for school—but then later sent her a text message that said "sry mom." Sadikman writes effusively:

> I'm grateful that my daughter reached out to me after our fraught start this morning. The only catch is, she's not supposed to be texting at school, especially during class. For a moment I wonder how she's getting away with it—Is her phone hidden under the desk? Is she texting from her muted laptop?— but I quickly let it go. I rarely initiate conversation with her during school hours unless it's urgent, but I won't ignore her texts to me. Despite the school's rules, I'm not going to miss this opportunity to connect with my girl.[6]

Sadikman may not be concerned with how her daughter managed to text her serendipitously, but she should be. The truth is that these constant interruptions in the classroom are making education harder.

And the fact that parents are enjoying these interactions is going to make them more difficult to end. I was recently engaged in a conversation with a mother of a seventh grader. Every couple of minutes we would be interrupted by a message coming through her phone. "Is everything okay?" I inquired. Oh yes, she assured me. It was just her daughter wanting to tell her about what was going on at school, what a friend of hers had said to her, and how her daughter had responded. "I just love being able to hear from her during the day," the mom gushed. The mother of a seventh-grade boy nearby interrupted to tell us she was jealous because her son never contacts her during the day. It makes you wonder whether parents wouldn't just rather keep their kids home so they can chat all day rather than send them off to be educated.

Chester E. Finn, a former assistant secretary of education, told me de Blasio's move is "truly outrageous from the teachers' perspective, as once they're allowed in the building . . . it becomes the teacher's job to police whether they're actually turned off, etc. As if the teacher had nothing else to police." Indeed, the teachers in disadvantaged schools already have plenty of other disruptions in their classes. Why should they have to compete with Androids and iPhones to get their classes' attention?

Christine Rosen, who writes about technology and culture for *New Atlantis*, tells me that "even if you set aside the issues of cyberbullying, cheating, and general distractedness that cell phones will abet, kids already spend most of their waking hours staring at screens. Shouldn't we try to preserve some spaces at school for the cultivation of other valuable skills, such as face-to-face communication and socializing?"

Some mothers have started to figure this out. Writing in the

*Washington Post,* Allison Slater Tate, a mother of four, tells the story of her eighth-grade son falling asleep on the bus home. A parent had texted her from the bus stop to tell her that her son had not gotten off with the other kids. She immediately called him, but no one picked up. After frantic calls to the school and the bus company, the bus driver found him. He was fast asleep, and his phone battery had died. Rather than lecture him about being more responsible with his phone, though, Tate came to a different conclusion about the way she had begun to think of his phone:

> The truth is, my children don't need to be reach-able every moment—even to me—to be safe. As our experience with the middle school bus showed me, a cell phone is no safety net, but other human beings are. My children are in a carpool with other parents I trust. They ride home on a school bus full of other children and a driver with a phone. They are at school all day with teachers and administrators charged with their care and well-being. They go to practices with coaches who can help them if they need it. Yes, I like the idea of being able to call them or text them at will, but at what cost to my children? Do my children deserve to be able to get lost sometimes, to figure things out for themselves, to allow the network of adults around them to do their jobs and be their safety net until they come back to me?[7]

Breonda has come to a similar conclusion. She tries to empha-size to her daughter that her phone and other kinds of tech-nology "are a tool, not a lifeline." She should surround herself with people who can help her if she needs it, and she should develop the kind of independence necessary to solve her own problems as well.

The idea that phones are merely tools is something that kids have trouble fathoming, in part because their parents are so inclined to see technology as a lifeline. For many, of course, it's a lifeline because it connects us to the office, though many of us have a tendency to overemphasize just how much we need to be connected. We may be checking our phones to see if there is an email from work, but while we're checking, we're distracted by items that are not urgent at all. Many of the parents I spoke to acknowledged that they needed to reevaluate their relationships to their devices before they could tell their children to limit their screen time.

And it's not just work that is forcing us to be staring at screens all the time. Phones have been a kind of lifeline for many stay-at-home mothers. They can check in with friends and family and share pictures of whatever it is they are doing with their kids without having to hire a babysitter. But some of the mothers I spoke with are starting to wonder whether smartphones are too distracting.

Danielle, a stay-at-home mother of four in Massachusetts, tells me that she thinks many mothers have a "high level of anxiety over phones. They are checking Facebook and Instagram because frankly there are a lot of adults who do that. Kids are just doing what Mom or Dad is doing too." While she says she is guilty of checking her phone while in line at the grocery store or at dinner if her companion goes to the bathroom, she says she doesn't check it on the playground. "It's a huge pet peeve." She has a Fitbit watch that she leaves on to check the time, but she leaves her phone in her bag. And she decided she doesn't need a smartphone either. "I don't have a job. I don't need to be checking my email. Do I need to know the Gap is having a sale?" Well, not immediately anyway.

Jeff Dill, a professor of sociology at Eastern University in Pennsylvania, has spent a lot of time interviewing parents about technology. A report he did called "The Culture of American Families"[8] started off just asking parents generally about their concerns: Did they think things were more difficult when they were kids? Or did their kids have things tougher? Without any prompting, parents kept mentioning the issues of technology.

"What drove me nuts more as a parent than as a social science observer," says Dill, is that "when we did interviews in people's homes—public housing projects and McMansions and everything in between—you would hear parents gripe and complain about technology. But then you look around the room and there are sixteen devices lying around."

Dill says his initial response was "Why don't you say no?" But now, having four sons of his own, he says that "limits are not as easy as we think. One of the hallmarks of modernity is that we always attempt to transcend limits—whether its familial bonds or technological ones." Still, he found that there were "simple things" parents didn't do to limit their kids' technology use. Mothers and fathers were often using devices to communicate with their kids who were in the next room.

Dill and his fellow researchers were able to distill the parents' concerns to a list of seven primary issues regarding technology. It is easy to see how the possession of cell phones by children seems to exacerbate all of these.

Technology, he found:

1. Normalized behaviors that are not normal, particularly the way that kids communicated with each other.
2. Made kids grow up too fast.
3. Increased the bullying and mean treatment of others.

4. Made it hard for parents to keep up with what their kids are doing.
5. Distracted from family time.
6. Inhibited outside play and engagement with the natural world.
7. Made it challenging for kids to distinguish between the real world and the virtual one.

Dill says that his oldest son at 13 has an iPod that he can play games on and a Kindle for reading books but still no ability to text message or place calls. Part of his concern is the content of what his kids could be receiving on a phone, but "the thing that gets overlooked," he says, is that "the medium is the message." He worries that children's "moral imaginations get shrunk or changed by devices." In the next chapter, we will examine more of the content that kids can find on their devices. But as Dill says, it is useful to think first about the medium.

In 2013, comedian Louis C.K. told Conan O'Brien about the problems with giving kids smartphones. "I think these things are toxic, especially for kids. They don't look at people when they talk to them, and they don't build empathy." Louis C.K. continued: "You know, kids are mean, and it's 'cause they're trying it out. They look at a kid and they go, 'you're fat,' and then they see the kid's face scrunch up and they go, 'oh, that doesn't feel good to make a person do that.' But they got to start with doing the mean thing. But when they write 'you're fat,' then they just go, 'mmm, that was fun, I like that.'"[9]

The instances of cyberbullying have only multiplied in recent years. Somehow the technology has so detached children from the feelings and actions of other people that they may be more likely to drive others to drastic measures. In

2017, Michelle Carter was convicted of manslaughter after authorities learned that she texted her boyfriend to "get back in" his truck as it was filling with carbon monoxide. "You can't think about it," Carter, who was seventeen at the time, texted him. "You just have to do it. You said you were gonna do it. Like I don't get why you aren't."[10] It's hard to imagine this kind of interaction happening in person.

But it's not cyberbullying that really gets Louis C.K., the father of two girls. It's the way that technology distracts us from real emotions. Louis C.K. described how you used to get into your car and hear a sad song and get depressed. But now, as soon as you get that feeling, you can just start texting your friends. "You're in your car, and you start going, 'Oh no, here it comes. That I'm alone.' It starts to visit on you. Just this sadness. Life is tremendously sad, just by being in it. That's why we text and drive."[11]

Rosen says, "It's not often we get a comedian channeling Blaise Pascal." But like the philosopher, Louis C.K. is saying, "If we all exist in a state of perpetual distraction, we'll never learn how to be alone." And we'll never learn how to deal with sadness. A friend recently told me the story of her son's friend who killed himself just before he was about to graduate from high school. Just before he took his life, he texted a picture of a gun to the girl who had recently broken up with him. My friend wondered whether teenagers today are simply lacking the ability to deal with disappointment and unhappiness. Forty years ago, if bad things happened, you eventually had to turn off the light and go to sleep. Now you can stay up all night online playing games, texting friends, doing anything to ensure that you don't have to think about what went wrong. We are not trained by life's small disappointments for its big ones.

On the flip side, technology can limit our experience of joy as well. Its effects may stunt our emotions so much that we will never get to experience the enjoyment that comes from being alone in the car as a great song comes on the radio and we belt it out as loud as we can. Wendy Mogel, author of *The Blessing of a Skinned Knee*, worries that the constant social interaction through technology "evens out our reactions in a way that doesn't help us build up muscles for joy or anguish or what to do to sustain ourselves" when those extreme emotions come upon us.

Our kids need to learn how to be alone with themselves *and* learn how to interact with others. While young people may see computers and phones as a vehicle for interacting with other people, they can also get in the way of those interactions. And in some ways, devices are replacing actual human interaction while making us believe we are more connected to others.

As movies like *Her*, the story of a relationship between a man and his operating system released in 2013, make clear, we now develop relationships with our technology instead of other people. We are seeking, as Sherry Turkle puts it, "the computer as an intimate machine."[12] And the cell phone, which we now take everywhere with us—to bed, to the bathroom, etc.—is as intimate as it gets.

In her book *Life on the Screen: Identity in the Age of the Internet*, Turkle interviews someone who was introduced to computer culture in the late '70s and saw it as "encouraging social isolation." "She had contempt 'for computer people' who were 'always working with their machines. . . . They run to computers as imaginary friends,'" she explained. As Turkle notes, today's high school students, on the other hand, are "more likely to think of computers as gateways to communication." But the first assessment may be the more correct one.[13]

Much of Turkle's work is devoted to seeing how human

beings interact with computers specifically. She has written extensively about ELIZA, for instance, a computer that was programmed to respond to human conversation as a kind of friend or therapist for its users. Developed by Joseph Weizenbaum, a scientist at MIT, as a kind of early example of natural language processing, people tried out ELIZA as a kind of experiment but quickly became attached to it.

Weizenbaum's secretary, who had watched him develop the code for ELIZA and realized that it was just a computer program, actually asked him to leave the room while she had a conversation with the computer because she felt it was too intimate. Weizenbaum concluded that "extremely short exposures to a relatively simple computer program could induce powerful delusional thinking in normal people."[14]

This delusional thinking extends to robots too, as Turkle documents in her 2011 book *Alone Together*. Here she documents the relationships that kids have with their "Furby" pets. These small furry robots, released in the early 2000s, became hugely popular, particularly because kids could teach them language skills. The kids that Turkle interviewed seemed both deeply attached to and also anxious about their robotic companions. As one girl tells Turkle, "Dolls let you tell them what you want. The Furbies have their own ideas." Turkle notes that traditional dolls can be "hard work" because they require your imagination.[15] The Furbies demanded a different kind of work. Not imagination, but constant attention. In this way, they are a lot like our online friendships.

Turkle argues that "sociable robots open new possibilities for narcissistic experience" because we are not really experiencing a relationship with another fully developed being. Children, in particular, she notes, "need to be with other people to develop mutuality and empathy; interacting with a robot cannot reach these."[16]

While the friends and classmates that our children are interacting with online are real people not robots, somehow their presence as only pictures or word bubbles on our screens makes them both more and less demanding than other relationships. On the one hand, they are always there, telling us what they want. On the other, they are one-dimensional. We think of their reactions as more of a reflection on us than anything substantive about them. And when we turn off our devices, they seem to disappear.

Rena, the mother of two preteen girls in New Jersey, gave her daughter a cell phone when she started middle school. She was doing extracurricular activities that made pickups and drop-offs more complicated, so the phone seemed convenient. Her daughter can text and call, but there is no social media. At nine, Rena takes the phone and plugs it in next to her own bed so there is no chance her daughter can use it at night. Her friends' parents do not have the same policy, as Rena often sees her daughter's phone buzzing with incoming texts at midnight or later. What this means is not just that the content of their conversations is probably going unmonitored. It's that the conversation never stops.

When kids have their own devices, they are tempted to be in touch constantly and maybe even feel obligated to be in touch when they don't want to. A ten- or eleven-year-old without a phone can simply tell her friends that she couldn't talk because she has to use a family computer or family phone in order to communicate. She can even say that she cannot be available after a certain time because her mother confiscates the phone. But once you have a phone, it is hard to ignore it. As in the adult world, not answering implies you are ignoring someone or something.

Mark Lerner, a clinical psychologist based in New York, says that he believes that many of the mental health issues young people are facing today can be traced to technology. He recalls being out on a fishing boat with his son. "He was looking at his iPhone and he said, 'Oh my God. Robin Williams just committed suicide.'" There is a constant stream of this kind of news that we simply can't get away from because we take our phones everywhere. Says Lerner, "These mechanisms of distribution are overwhelming us with information." They are taking a toll on adults, but, as Lerner notes, they are even worse for children.

So much of our job as parents is helping kids to keep the events of their lives in perspective. Sure we have big first birthday celebrations and are thrilled when they learn to walk and graduate from diapers. Of course we want to celebrate their highs and offer sympathy for their lows. But our job is often to say—as my grandmother did—"This too shall pass." We can't let them think that they are set for life because they got an A on their math quiz. But we also can't let them think that life is over because a friend got mad at them. Because we have lived longer and have some sense of which events are big and which are small, we can pass along this important information to them.

But it is hard to distinguish, as many adults realize, what is important and what is not when the information is coming in through phones. People use text messages instead of email because they pop up on a screen immediately. They have the sense of urgency about them—even when they just say, "Hey, What's up?"

In his book *Amusing Ourselves to Death*, Neil Postman writes that we live in a "peek-a-boo world, where now this event, now that, pops into view for a moment, then vanishes again. It is a world without much coherence or sense, a world that does not ask us, indeed, does not permit us to do anything; a world that is, like the child's game of peek-a-boo, entirely self-contained. But like peek-a-boo, it is also endlessly entertaining."[17]

> Play the memory game. If you're tempted to give kids technology because you can't figure out how else they would entertain themselves or communicate with you or their friends, ask yourself how you did it as a kid. The answer won't always be the right one, but it will give you perspective.

Postman probably never could have imagined the peek-a-boo worlds of our Facebook feeds, in which a celebrity's death is listed just after the birth of a cousin's baby, where an article about a school shooting in another state appears after pictures from the kids' soccer game. Some of these things are of great importance, some less so. Very few of them affect us directly. But when they come in through a phone, they all seem pressing. And many of them seem to demand an immediate response.

Giving kids cell phones may give parents peace of mind, but they also make kids more anxious. This has effects that are deeply harmful in some very obvious ways. In his book *The Collapse of Parenting*, psychiatrist Leonard Sax describes how parents have come to see him complaining that their kids were not able to focus at school. These mothers and fathers had assumed that it was because of ADHD or some other medical disorder and were looking for him to prescribe some medication. With a little probing, Sax found that the kids were texting their friends well into the night without their parents' knowledge, missing out on valuable hours of sleep.[18] These kids felt compelled to stay connected as long as possible because they didn't want to be the last one to know what was going on.

Kids want to be in the loop even if what's going on is totally unimportant. In an essay he wrote for *Acculturated*, Mark Bauerlein explained how adolescents today can surround themselves entirely with media that feature them. They can go from texting and using social media to watching television programming that revolves around them entirely. Not only does this encourage a level of narcissism unknown to previous generations, but it makes it very hard for them to keep the dramas of their lives in any kind of perspective.[19]

This is one reason that researchers have found higher levels of narcissism among young people today. Research by Jean Twenge found that scores on the Narcissistic Personality Inventory (NPI) increased about 30 percent among college students between the 1980s and early 2000s.[20] She found similar results for high school students. It's not just the helicopter parents praising kids for every small accomplishment or the self-esteem movement taking over schools and promising each child that he or she is special. It's also technology. Most obviously, it's the selfie. How can you take dozens of pictures of yourself a day and not become more self-involved?

But technology produces more than just individual narcissism. It creates generational blinders. Anyone who is outside of your immediate age range is no longer in your line of sight. So much time is spent keeping up with the drama of friends and schoolmates, and technology means that it can never be turned off.

In 2015, a team of childhood development experts worked with CNN to survey the social media postings of two hundred thirteen-year-olds from across the country. After combing through more than 150,000 posts (from Twitter, Instagram,

Facebook, etc.), the experts concluded that, as Anderson Cooper put it, being thirteen is like a "real-time 24-7 popularity competition."[21]

Maybe that doesn't sound so much different from what you remember of middle school, but the resulting documentary, *#Being13: Inside the Secret World of Teens*, will seem deeply troubling to anyone over the age of thirty. First, of course, there's the frequency with which teens are on mobile devices. The boys and girls interviewed acknowledged checking them more than one hundred times a day. Sometimes two hundred.

When the producers at CNN asked parents to take their kids' phones away for a couple of days, the kids went berserk. One mother recorded her daughter's screams and tears. "I would rather not eat for a week than get my phone taken away," said Gia. "When I get my phone taken away, I feel kind of naked," said Kyla. "I do feel kind of empty without my phone."

While the experts were reluctant to call this "addiction," at least in any medical sense, the parents weren't. In a focus group interview with mothers and fathers of eight of the teens, all readily agreed that their teens were addicted. One father described how his son became a completely different person for weeks—withdrawn and depressed—when his phone was taken away.

▪ ▪ ▪ ▪

When it comes to technology, parents must examine not only how they want their children to relate to the devices or how much of their time they want kids to spend texting or emailing or gaming or surfing. They need to decide something more fundamental—how their children are going to interact with the rest of the world.

It is not an exaggeration to say that giving your kids a cell phone is giving them the keys to the kingdom. There is a whole world out there that they can now access without your knowledge. That world, which will be constantly beeping at your child, will forever change him or her. It may change how your child views friendships, how he or she interacts with the outdoors, how he or she experiences time alone.

When we hand over phones and tablets to children, we are likely to be changing not only the information they can access but also their habits, their personalities, and their tastes. And while they may see their online life as a privilege—if not a right—we should also be honest enough to understand it as a burden. For the sake of our own convenience and their entertainment, we are giving up their freedom and perhaps even some of their happiness.

## CHAPTER 5

# The Price of Internet Access
# Is Eternal Vigilance

■ ■ ■ ■

"WITH MY daughters, I worry about the 'mean girls' stuff. With my son, I worry about the porn." That was a father of three outside Cleveland explaining his concerns about his kids and technology. Indeed, most of the parents I interviewed offered a similar assessment. When it came to their girls, they were anxious about all the pressures associated with social media—the magnification of bullying by the constant presence of technology—and when it came to their sons, they wondered how to keep a lid on the most graphic images—both sexual and violent—on the Internet.

Boys and girls have very different relationships with technology. And so, for that matter, do mothers and fathers. In almost all of my interviews, mothers reported being more concerned about how much screen time their kids had than fathers did. Fathers were much more likely to be the ones purchasing the devices and allowing kids to use them. Danielle tells me that she and her husband had agreed to purchase Kindle Fires for their four children for Christmas, but when they went on sale months before, he went ahead and bought them. One day, Danielle came home to find all four children (under the age of eight), glued to his or her very own device. "If they get bored," she says, "his answer is usually to give them a device or a phone, much quicker than I ever would."

Even though Erin says she and her husband both grew

up having their television viewing severely restricted, he is much more likely to let the kids (age eight and six) to take pictures on a phone or show them a short video here or there. Amy, who has been divorced for five years and has three children, ages twenty-two, eighteen, and eight, says that her ex-husband tends to be more indulgent with technology than she is—both in giving devices to the kids and giving them more time to use them.

In their defense, many of these fathers grew up playing video games themselves and some of them tell me they do not see much harm in their kids doing the same. They would spend hours in front of Nintendo with their friends and they still managed to get good grades and become successful adults. How much has changed in the intervening years? The graphics on video games have gotten much more realistic, the games can now involve contact with strangers or classmates online, and the games can be played on mobile devices, meaning they can be played all the time.

Adam Cox, a clinical psychologist in Southern California, tells me that the boys and girls he sees have completely different experiences with technology:

> I think boys are just completely infatuated by the kind of trickery of technology. I don't get that from school-age girls. When was the last time I heard a tween girl say she couldn't wait to go home and play Xbox with her mom? Never. But that's what quality time is between boys and dads. The dads are into it too. Whether it's a virtual reality experience or a combat game or a car race.

While Cox understands the inclination, he worries that video games are "less effortful play than other kinds of things fathers used to do with their sons like going to playground to play catch or going for a bike ride."

A few years ago, I went to hear Rosalind Wiseman talk about her book *Masterminds and Wingmen*. She advised a packed audience of New York City parents not to worry so much about their sons playing video games, or at least to understand that they are not psychopaths for wanting to do so. The latter sentiment, anyway, seems perfectly reasonable. But parents—both mothers and fathers—do worry about the realism and violence in some of the video games.

Duncan, an elementary school principal and the father of a high school-age son, says he and his wife both worried about the graphic nature of some video games. "First-person shooter games," where the player is staring down the barrel of a gun, were not allowed when his son was younger. Perhaps this restriction is the influence of Columbine and other school shootings on these parents' attitudes. They simply do not want their kid to be able to simulate looking through the sights of a gun and then picking off enemies.

Duncan says some of his son's friends were playing games that were rated M (for mature audiences) when they were in second grade, but his son knew he was not allowed. Not only did Duncan worry about the graphic nature of these games, he didn't like scenarios where they were "shooting Arabs." Now that his son is older, he wants him to make his own decisions about these matters.

In 2013, *Grand Theft Auto V* made a record $1 billion during its first three days on the market. According to Common Sense Media, *Grand Theft Auto V* is

> brimming with gang violence, nudity, extremely coarse language, and drug and alcohol abuse. It isn't a game for kids. Playing as hardened criminals,

players kill not only fellow gangsters but also police officers and innocent civilians using both weapons and vehicles while conducting premeditated crimes, including a particularly disturbing scene involving torture. Women are frequently depicted as sexual objects, with a strip club mini-game allowing players to fondle strippers' bodies, which are nude from the waist up. Players also have the opportunity to make their avatars use marijuana and drink alcohol, both of which impact their perception of the world.[1]

The site concludes, "None of the main characters in the game makes for a decent role model." No kidding.

So who is playing this video game? A study found that online players of *Grand Theft Auto V* are 33 percent more likely to have children and are twice as likely to be married as the average video game player. They are also 54 percent more likely to be middle class.[2] While the group that conducted the study marveled at these statistics, the truth is that many of these parents were probably playing the games with their teenagers or they were allowing their teens to play with them.

Amy says she is shocked by the graphic nature of some of the games her eight-year-old son has seen at other kids' homes. She tells me: "There's a thing called *Five Nights at Freddy's*. It's the scariest video game ever. There are animated toys that try to kill you. My son saw it and now he's in therapy. It's horrifying. He's scared to go into the bathroom. They can't unsee these things."

The question remains, though, whether these video games have any effect on kids' behavior. In a 2014 article in *JAMA Pediatrics*, Craig Anderson, director of the Center for the Study of Violence at Iowa State University, and his colleagues found that playing violent video games may encourage more hostile thoughts in children and, as a result, more aggressive actions.[3] A study of more than three thousand kids in elementary and middle school in Singapore found that kids who played more hours of violent video games were more likely to say it was acceptable for a boy to hit another kid if that kid said something negative about him. They also were more likely to say they would be aggressive if they were provoked, even accidentally. Those who had played violent video games for a long time were also more likely to fantasize about hitting someone they didn't like.

Speaking to *Time* magazine, Anderson explained, "What this study does is show that it's media violence exposure that is teaching children and adolescents to see the world in a more aggressive kind of way." Says Anderson: "It shows very strongly that repeated exposure to violent video games can increase aggression by increasing aggressive thinking."[4]

But Christopher Ferguson, a professor of psychology at Stetson University, has mined studies on video games and kids, including Anderson's, and concluded that violent video games do not produce violent behavior. He has written that

> even while video game sales have skyrocketed, youth violence plummeted to its lowest levels in 40 years. . . . Secondly, it has been increasingly recognized that much of the early research on VVG [violent video games] linking them to increased aggression was problematic: most studies used outcome measures that had nothing to do with real-life aggression and failed to control carefully for other important variables, such as family violence, mental health issues or even gender in many studies (boys both play more VVG and are more aggressive).[5]

Ferguson tells me that kids would have to be spending at least six hours a day on a screen for media to have the slightest effect on them (which is not exactly impossible, looking at average daily screen time among kids these days). Those effects include mental health issues like depression and attention problems as well as risky behaviors like violence, smoking, and substance abuse. Ferguson believes that "you'd have to really work at it to screw your kid up with media. Maybe if you put your three-year-old in front of a Quentin Tarantino movie," he says. He notes that many of the biggest problems kids face today are "because of their family environments, their peers, or other mental health issues." Media use, he argues, is often a symptom of a problem, not the problem itself.

And he is right to some degree. It is hard to separate kids' use of media from other aspects of their environments. You don't need a psychologist to tell you that parents are going to have more of an influence over kids' behavior and attitudes than anything they see on a screen.

Ferguson is one of those people who says we need to calm down about technology because we have seen this all before. He tells me, "People thought trains would be the end of civilization. We freak out over any change in society. But society adjusts. There are just different ways of doing things."

Despite his reserve in the face of these changes, Ferguson acknowledges that it is useful to think about "what kids could be doing instead of" consuming media. "Kids can't play video games sixteen hours a day and be successful. You have to make sure they're getting exercise, doing homework, spending time with their families. They need to spend time with Mom and Dad and their peers. They need to be spending more time outside."

Ferguson thinks games like *Halo* (a military-style, first-person shooter game) are okay for kids, and if a father wants to bond with his son by playing *Halo* for three hours that's okay too. "You are taking technology and integrating it into your life rather than it being an isolating activity." Like many parents, Ferguson is a fan of *Minecraft*: "It's a cultural phenomenon. It's very well constructed because you can do so many things and exercise your creativity. It's flexible." But he doesn't see much qualitative difference between *Minecraft* and *Grand Theft Auto* as far as kids' development is concerned.

While it is useful to think about Ferguson's measures of whether video games are affecting our kids' behavior and even their emotional states, it is also good to think of whether our goals as parents go beyond ensuring that our kids are not violent, depressed, or failing academically.

The psychologist Adam Cox says that the major effects he sees of technology on kids are a loss of empathy and a loss of ability to slow down the mind. The two are related, though, because the reason kids don't have empathy is because they have lost the ability "to consider what others want from you." It's a kind of "emotional intelligence" that is developed through careful thought. While we take it for granted as adults—it becomes instinctual—kids are still considering each situation. And in adolescence, those situations become more complicated.

But slowing down is just too boring for them, Cox notes, after they have spent so much time getting immediate gratification from a screen. "Kids who have been raised on technology can feel physically ill when they are not being stimulated. They have translated boredom into physical distress." For example, kids whose phones have been taken away and who are away from video games or social media often complain of having stomachaches, he says. Cox, who has been seeing children at his practice since 2000, says he first became aware of this problem around 2006. "A child feels that all the time: My brain will consist of all peaks and no valleys. It's like someone who lives on cocaine."

Unlike reading a book or playing a board game or even sports, where there are moments for stopping and thinking, video games seem to consolidate time. "It's like constantly being on a roller coaster," without having a moment to stop and catch your breath, says Cox. Even if your child is not becoming more violent or doing poorly in school, this kind of mental training will have an effect on their temperament, and not necessarily for the better.

## Tips for Cutting Back

Ban the phrase "I'm bored." There is enough stuff to do in any twenty-first-century American home to prevent boredom. Send your kids outside for at least a half an hour. Teach them a new card game. Tell them to read a book. If they can't find anything entertaining, there are dishes to load and laundry to fold.

In their book *Imagination and Play in the Electronic Age*, research psychologists Dorothy Singer and Jerome Singer argue that the "research findings for violent video game playing certainly seem ominous." And while they seem to accept a great deal of the research on the effects violent video games can have on kids' behavior, they also express other concerns: "The narrow scope of imagination fostered by violent video games may put habitual players at risk not only for developing aggressive personalities or showing antisocial behavior, but also for limiting their imaginative repertoire and scholastic interests."[6]

The idea that video games can restrict imagination and creativity is a concern that comes up with regard to the effects of technology generally. In their book *The App Generation*, Howard Gardner and Katie Davis attempt to look at the fiction writing and artwork of young people today to understand how their creative products have changed over time. Comparing stories written by middle schoolers in the early '90s with those written in 2011, the two note that in the latter the plots were more linear, their subjects were more typically drawn from everyday life and involved fewer fantasy elements, and their language was less varied and included more expletives. And while the artwork the authors examined certainly was less conventional, it often involved "remixing," which is to say there was less original work in the creations even if students were putting art or music together in new ways.[7]

Gardner and Davis write, "Individuals generate new ideas by reflecting on the world that surrounds them. Reflection requires attention and time (counterintuitive as it may initially seem, boredom has long been a powerful stimulator of the imagination), two things that are hard to come by in today's media-saturated world."[8]

But the violent video games seem to do more than inhibit the imagination. The Singers note that "boys may show less willingness to put in the time needed to master the sequential and focused cognitive and small-motor skills they will need in society, where women will increasingly be their effective rivals."[9] It is interesting to think that boys might be put at more of a disadvantage academically because of their attachment to video games, but as we will see shortly, girls' use of social media may have equally deleterious effects on their well-being.

The preferences for different kinds of technology for girls and boys become more pronounced during the teen years.

But the more you dig into the effect of technology on adolescence, the more you realize how much crossover there is. Maureen, a mother, tells me about how her son, a senior in high school, sometimes gets depressed when he goes on to social media. He has friends but he's "an introvert," she tells me. During the summer, he would see other kids getting together without him and he would get depressed. One day she handed him a note card with a list of "ten things you could do instead of being on Facebook." They included calling a friend, reading a book to his sister, going to the mall with a friend. "When I handed him the card, his face lit up." He got his younger sisters and played *Let's Dance* on their Wii. While we traditionally associate girls with the fear of missing out (FOMO) that comes from seeing friends on social media, boys care about this stuff too.

But there are differences. Psychiatrist Leonard Sax describes in the *New York Times* the typical teenagers he sees. Parents will bring in their sixteen-year-old son. "He's not working hard at school and his grades are sliding. . . . He spends most of his free time playing video games like *Grand Theft Auto* or *Call of Duty*, or surfing the Web for pictures of girls. He's happy as a clam."[10]

On the other hand is their daughter, age fourteen, who is a straight-A student, an athlete, and has many friends. But when I met with her, she told me that she isn't sleeping well. She wakes up in the middle of the night, feeling remorseful about having eaten a whole slice of pizza for dinner. She often has shortness of breath. Recently she has begun cutting herself with razor blades on her upper inner thigh, where her parents won't see. She hasn't told her parents any of this. On the surface, she is the golden girl. Inside, she is falling apart.[11]

Sax believes that the greater anxiety girls experience today has to do with social media. "Imagine another girl sitting in her bedroom, alone. She's scrolling through other girls' Instagram and Snapchat feeds. She sees Sonya showing off her new bikini; Sonya looks awesome. She sees Madison at a party, having a blast. She sees Vanessa with her adorable new puppy. And she thinks: *I'm just sitting here in my bedroom, not doing anything. My life sucks.*" Teenage girls have always been more concerned about their looks, but now there is not a moment of the day when they won't be able to compare themselves to their classmates.[12]

A big chunk of our cultural discussion about the ill effects of technology on children begins with adolescence, though perhaps it should begin much sooner. This is because we can easily see how—thanks in part to the overuse of technology—teenagers are not turning into the young men and women we hope and expect them to be. But we also tend to focus on adolescence because that is where we see the worrisome intersection of technology and sex. It certainly starts younger, but the parents I interviewed seem to suggest that the age of twelve is when they realize how the Internet is affecting their kids' relationships and also how it's helping them to shape their own identity, sexual and otherwise.

Parents are comparing their own teenage lives with those of their children and they're nervous. As one mother in the sub-urbs of Boston put it to me, "We did stupid things or embar-rassed ourselves in high school. We told the wrong person a secret. But it wasn't on your permanent footprint for rest of your life." Even if these kids don't do anything stupider than their parents or grandparents did, the consequences will still be worse.

It is not uncommon to hear researchers and pundits like Christopher Ferguson say that when it comes to technology, there is really nothing new under the sun. A senior researcher at Microsoft and author of *It's Complicated: The Social Lives of*

*Networked Teens,* danah boyd, writes, "None of the capabilities enabled by social media are new." She encourages readers to calm down about teens' use of Facebook, Twitter, and the like and notes that if you wanted to spread rumors about someone else before our modern age, it was pretty easy to do: "Messages printed in the school newspaper or written on bathroom walls have long been visible."[13] She is regularly interviewed by news outlets like NPR to discuss such matters.

But it's not just tech boosters like boyd (Would Microsoft still pay her if she were more sanguine about the effects of technology on kids?) who have this attitude. I was on a panel with contributors to the conservative magazine *National Review* in the summer of 2015. One of them noted that "people used to say that motels" were going to undermine public morality too. The idea is that each generation sees something that it believes will fundamentally alter society—or even human nature. Whether it's comic books or radio or motels, we have always had new technologies disrupting our lives. Why should the Internet be any different? We have already talked about the ways in which watching television and playing games on screens have changed the experience of childhood.

But it is obviously more than just the screens themselves. There are three fundamental ways in which the Internet has changed the experience of adolescence—for the worse. Let's call them "the three Ps" for short.

First, what our children do online is *private.* More and more parents have found out the hard way that even with all the monitoring they do, it is not enough. Teens are able to surf the web and communicate with their friends using programs and apps that we simply don't even know exist. Filters cannot prevent this. Indeed, a 2017 study by researchers at Oxford University found that "the use of internet filtering in the home did not appear to mitigate the risk of young people having unpleasant online experiences and that technical ability to bypass these filters had no observed effect on the likelihood of such experiences."[14]

According to my survey, almost 90 percent of parents think they are good or very good at monitoring their kids' use of technology. But that confidence level falls significantly as children get older. Indeed, if their oldest child is between thirteen and seventeen, 47 percent of respondents believe their children are hiding things they're doing online. According to a 2016 survey carried out by security firm Kaspersky Lab, 42 percent of ten-year-olds believe they have the technological capability to hide things online from their parents.[15]

## Tips for Cutting Back

Keep all devices in public places. Even if your child would rather watch the iPad in bed or play on a phone with the door closed, get them in the habit of assuming that you can always see what they're doing. And so can everyone else.

Second, what our children do online is *public*. Anyone can find out where they've been online and what they've been doing. In fact, their friends will probably have an easier time finding out than their parents. But as they get older, they will find that anything that has been put in an email or on social media has the potential to be shared with others. The digital footprint that they have developed—or the one that has been developed for them with the help of parents who have snapped photos and written posts about them since birth—is not safe from prying eyes.

Finally, what our children do online is *permanent*. In 2014, Europe's highest court ruled that citizens have a "right to be forgotten." As Farhad Manjoo writes in the *New York Times*, "Privacy advocates cheered the decision . . . which seemed to offer citizens some recourse to what had become a growing menace of modern life: The Internet never forgets, and, in its robotic zeal to collect and organize every scrap of data about everyone, it was beginning to wreak havoc on personal privacy."[16] Well, obviously. But it's very hard to see how this ruling is enforceable. Links go up, come down, and go up somewhere else. How is it possible to ensure that search engines never link to inaccurate or hurtful information? It's not. But if this is a message that adults don't seem to understand—or at least don't consider when they're about to send an email or post something on social media—how do we expect our kids to?

## Tips for Cutting Back

Email is forever. Just as you teach your kids to save their documents when they're writing a school report, make sure they understand that much of what they write will never really disappear. And it could come back to haunt them later.

A friend told me a story about a pastor he knew who decided to print the Facebook pages of some of the teens in his congregation, supersizing them on enormous sheets of poster board and putting them up around the sanctuary. When the kids walked in, they were outraged that the pastor would put up their private thoughts for the whole world to see. Which was exactly the point.

As adults we often wonder what adolescents (and even some other adults, ahem) are thinking when they post personal details of their lives on social networking websites. Don't they know that potential bosses and even other parents can read all that information?

The effects can be even more immediate. According to a 2016 survey by Kaplan Test Prep, 40 percent of college admissions officers report checking applicants' social media when they're weighing decisions about who should get an acceptance letter. That's four times the percentage who checked in 2008.[17]

About a third of these admissions officials say they've Googled an applicant to learn more about them. And those are only the ones who admit it. Perhaps this seems perfectly natural. After all, who among us hasn't met someone new—a date, a coworker, a friend—and decided to find out a little more about them online? What's amazing is that college admissions officers already have an entire dossier on their applicants. Not only do they know grade point averages and lists of extracurricular activities, but in many cases they have access to extensive financial records and personal family details.

So why do they also need to check out teens' social media pages? Sometimes they're looking merely to verify the information a student has submitted—whether it's awards received or information about a disciplinary or criminal record. Sometimes they're visiting social media pages at a student's invitation. Indeed, 42 percent of admissions officers say that students have asked them to come look at evidence of a special talent through their Facebook page or something similar.

But then there's what Kaplan refers to as "admissions sabotage," in which admissions officers "say they occasionally get anonymous tips about prospective students pointing them towards inappropriate behavior. They'll sometimes dig online to see if it has merit."[18]

Sadly, despite the warnings of parents and teachers, many kids pay no attention to the potential audience for their postings. When danah boyd asked one student about the possibility of teachers looking at her Facebook page, the girl responded: "Why are they on my page? I wouldn't go to my teacher's page and look at their stuff, so why should they go online to look at my stuff?"[19]

Boyd suggests that adults have left teens with few outlets for other kinds of social interaction and so they are using social media in order to make up for it. Our helicopter parenting, compulsion to overschedule our children's lives, and deepest fears about "stranger danger" have meant that teens do a lot less hanging out than they used to.

If they can't get to the mall, they congregate online—or so the reasoning goes. As Heather, one sixteen-year-old in Iowa, told boyd, "I can't really see people in person. I can barely hang out with my friends on the weekend, let alone people I don't talk to as often. I'm so busy. I've got lots of homework. I'm busy with track, I've got a job." As boyd explains, "For Heather, social media is not only a tool; it is a social lifeline that enables her to stay connected to people she cares about but cannot otherwise interact with in person."[20]

So teens see social media as the online equivalent of the mall. It's a public space where they nonetheless expect some privacy. They're not sitting in their parents' kitchen. They're not having a conversation outside the teachers' lounge. When they're walking around a public space with their friends, it's unlikely that someone is eavesdropping on them. But just as teens would probably end the conversation at the mall if they saw a group of their friends' parents sitting at the next table, they should probably think about changing their expectations of privacy on Facebook.

Many of the parents that boyd interviews see it as their responsibility to hover. But she warns them against this. And occasionally she has the facts on her side. She explains to parents that the dangers for their children online do not come from some preponderance of predators. Just like there aren't a lot of pedophiles hanging around your local park or kidnappers lurking at the mall's food court, there is not a high likelihood that your child will be victimized by a stranger online. "Internet-initiated sexual assaults," she writes, "are rare. The overall number of sex crimes against minors has been steadily declining since 1992, which also suggests that the Internet is not creating a new plague."[21]

In this area, as in other topics, boyd suggests that the Internet has not fundamentally altered human nature. It is merely a new technology reflecting the same old realities. But if boyd is helpful in calming excessive fears, her brisk reassurances are ultimately unpersuasive. She makes the age-old argument that if you don't let teens have some independence, they won't make the right choices when they are finally given some freedom. "Parents often engage in these acts out of love," she writes, "but fail to realize how surveillance is a form of oppression that limits teens' ability to make independent choices."[22]

Irritatingly, she never addresses what really is different about the Internet—and why even reasonable parents are inclined to hover. The Internet has brought material into our homes through the back door that we never would have allowed through the front. It is nothing less than shocking that boyd includes only one mention of the word "pornography" in her entire book. And that single mention is part of a long list of things that the public has "angst" about.

According the Crimes Against Children Research Center at

the University of New Hampshire, 42 percent of online users ages ten to seventeen had seen pornography, and 66 percent of those had seen it unwittingly, as a result of pop-up ads or something similar. Many of the parents of boys I interviewed said that their children had already encountered such images before middle school. Some parents tried to have a talk with their sons ahead of time but were at a loss about what to say.

## *Tips for Cutting Back*

Filters don't work. You can spend thousands of dollars getting someone to childproof your computers and it might not do a bit of good. If your child is on the Internet, they're on the whole Internet. Parents are the only real filters.

Julia Kim doesn't see this is as a problem that is likely to be solved any time soon. Kim, who has worked in technology both for the private sector and the government, says, first, it's simply a matter of the nature of the Internet. "All the things around the Internet started as a way to make information open, to make it challenging to control access." Information wants to be free, and so does pornography apparently.

The other problem, says Kim, is that "companies like Google and YouTube have become our gateways to the Internet. It's up to them to help or not help and it's presumably not in their interest so far to limit access to this kind of material." Parents may be a lucrative market, but this would be an expensive project. Kim says, "Companies just don't have enough of an incentive to come up with an effective kind of filter yet."

Which presents parents with a serious problem. In an essay for the *Daily Mail*, the former editor of a lad magazine called *Loaded* described his shock when he visited a class of thirteen- and fourteen-year-olds in the north of England. A researcher asked the kids questions about what they had viewed online. And without exception, these middle-class white boys and girls were very familiar with the pornography genre. I'll spare you most of the details (there was actually a term they all knew for sex with a woman who had no arms or legs), but they knew about things that even the researcher was unsure of. They reported that they were sent links to these pictures, videos, and such (whether they wanted them or not) via social networking sites.[23]

It is not uncommon to hear adults talk about how they looked at pornography when they were kids, but as most people who have spent any time online quickly realize, *Playboy* and *Hustler* from 1985 have little to do with what's online today. In her 2016 book *American Girls*, Nancy Jo Sales offers an overview of this world. In addition to child pornography and pornography in which adults are made to look under-age, there is also violence. "Rape and gang rape are common scenarios in online porn." A site called Rapetube actually encourages users to submit videos of sexual attacks for the titillation of others. Some were staged but others, according to experts, were probably real.[24]

In a book about how parents should approach technology, I would be remiss if I didn't give readers a sense of just how disturbing this material is. The idea that you should let your child go online until you walk in on them watching something disturbing—or you find it in their browser history—and then scold them about it, is naïve at best. The kind of videos we are talking about here simply cannot be unseen.

As Peggy Orenstein writes in her book, *Girls and Sex*,

whether it's "oral sex aimed at making women vomit," "multiple men ejaculating on a woman's face," or the 41 percent of videos in one study that were "ass to mouth," there is little question that today's pornography is offering boys a different view of sex than their fathers and grandfathers had. Writes Orenstein, "I'm going to go out on a limb and say that in real life those practices wouldn't feel good to most women. Watching natural-looking people engaging in sex that is consensual, mutually pleasurable and realistic may not be harmful . . . but that is not what the $97 billion global porn industry is shilling." Rather, Orenstein notes, "its producers have only one goal: to get men off hard and fast for profit. The most efficient way to do so appears to be eroticizing the degradation of women."[25]

But it is not just the content of pornography that is different for this generation. It is also its availability. Imagine the lengths to which a fourteen-year-old boy had to go in order to procure only one pornographic VHS tape, say, thirty years ago and then find a place to view it privately. Now compare that with what's available online. And then remember that can be accessed with the click of a button on a mobile device 24/7.

If there is any doubt that viewing these kinds of images with this kind of regularity has been having an effect on real life,

## Tips for Cutting Back

The price of the Internet is eternal vigilance. Filters are not going to prevent your children from accessing things you don't want them to see. If you think your kids are ready for a smartphone or access to Snapchat, you will have to monitor them.

just spend some time talking to girls in high school. Indeed, while Stetson University psychologist Christopher Ferguson notes that violence has not increased among young people despite the prevalence of violent video games, it does seem that certain kinds of sexual activity and expectations have changed due to the ubiquity of pornography.

High school girls are deeply aware of the "competition"—even if it's imaginary. Waxing their nether regions has become de rigueur. And, as Orenstein notes, anal sex has become such a common request that it is now referred to as "fifth base." According to the *New York Times*, "The American Society for Aesthetic Plastic Surgery says that 400 girls 18 and younger had labiaplasty last year, an 80 percent increase from the 222 girls who had cosmetic genital surgery in 2014."[26] It doesn't take Sherlock Holmes to figure out where boys formed their expectations for how girls should look and behave.

In their book *Premarital Sex in America*, sociologists Mark Regnerus and Jeremy Uecker cite pornography as a major source of sexual "information" for teenagers and young adults today.[27] As Regnerus tells me, "If [there] is a constant flow of this kind of sexual imagery, then girls learn what they're for and boys learn what girls are for too."

Pornography has warped what Regnerus and Uecker refer to as the "sexual marketplace." One young man they interviewed talked enthusiastically about digital porn. "I think I like my own 'personal time' as much as I like having intercourse." Regnerus and Uecker write that "if porn-and-masturbation satisfies some of the male demand for intercourse—and it clearly does—it reduces the value of real intercourse, access to which women control."[28] With the supply of sexual outlets rising, the "cost of real sex can only go down, taking men's interest in making steep relationship commitments with it."

Indeed, while the last decade has seen a decline in the rate of teenage pregnancy and perhaps even the rate of teenage intercourse, the lack of commitment in teen relationships seems to be a growing problem. And the expectations of what girls will do seem to be rising. Reading the landscape described by Sales and Orenstein, one sees the natural results of the "hook-up culture" trickling down to the high school and middle school level. Any time a teenage girl is alone in a room with a boy, the expectation seems to be that she will be offering him oral sex. Surely this is not universally true, but Orenstein, for one, seems struck by the inability of these otherwise smart, ambitious young women to turn down these "favors" that boys are asking.

"SEND NOODZ" is apparently a regular text that girls across the country receive from boys they know. These are girls from places like Montclair, New Jersey, where Sales finds that not only do some girls get these requests multiple times a day, but often they are flattered—or worried that if they don't they will be labeled prudes—and decide to comply.[29]

As Orenstein also writes, "Among the girls I met, the badgering to send nude photos could be incessant, beginning in middle school. One girl described how, in eighth grade, a male classmate threatened (in a text) to commit suicide if she didn't send him a picture of her breasts." The girl told her parents but another girl he tried this on actually complied.[30]

It would be a mistake, though, to say that these pictures are only coming at the requests of boys. One 2015 survey estimated that millennials will take more than twenty-five thousand pictures of themselves (selfies) during their lifetimes. The 2015 documentary *#Being13* provides a fascinating illustration of this process, with middle school kids explaining to interviewers how they prepare for each shot, how they decide which ones to post, and when, if they post the wrong one, it could seriously diminish their reputation at school.

Orenstein watches as these adolescents find the perfect pose—the one that will make them look thin and sexy, without looking slutty. She sees them so often that she can name them. At a Miley Cyrus concert, Orenstein stood next to a life-size poster of the singer where more than thirty different girls took pictures to post on social media. "A few made 'duck lips' or 'faux surprise' face—*I'm fun! I'm ironic!*—but most imitated their idol." They posed with a look they described to Orenstein as "I guess it's to say, 'I don't care.'" Even though they obviously do.[31]

And many girls are sending much more provocative pictures, without the slightest provocation from boys. More than one mother of a middle school boy has expressed concern that these girls seem "very fast." Here's a description that my friend Amy Anderson, the mother of two high school boys, writes from the front lines:

> One sunny June morning, as I sat in the plush chair of my neighborhood nail salon and luxuriated in the warm water bathing my feet, I picked up my iPhone and noticed a new app—"Kik"—that my 14-year-old son must have installed after losing his phone and hijacking mine for a few days. Out of curiosity, I pressed the icon. Up popped a hi-def picture of a young woman's unadorned crotch, with the message: "Hi!" . . . Horrified, I texted back: "PLEASE do not send images like this to my son or anybody else." The response arrived immediately: "Shuuuut UP! You're not funny!" Apparently, whomever this young woman was thought that I was my son.[32]

Presumably this particular image didn't make it any further than Anderson's phone. But most of these images do. They're traded like Pokémon cards among younger and older boys. Sales suggests that older boys will procure alcohol for younger ones in exchange for "noodz."[33]

It seems like an unending string of sexting scandals have occurred in recent years. In the fall of 2015, authorities in Cañon City, Colorado, discovered a sexting ring. At least a hundred students had been trading hundreds of nude photos. In an interview on public radio, the superintendent of the district, George Welsh, at first thought that the students who had been trading photos probably didn't realize the implications of their actions and needed someone to explain it to them. "Kids just don't get when you share this with one person you've lost all control."

But then, he said, he had an "Archie Bunker moment." Like the protagonist on *All in the Family*, Welsh told his interviewer, "Maybe time has passed me by. Meathead [Archie's son-in-law] says human bodies are beautiful and why can't a person if they choose to . . . why can't they share it with someone else?" Welsh said: "I don't have the answer."[34] Someone in Welsh's position might think to suggest that parents need to do a better job monitoring their kids. And if they can't, then their kids shouldn't have these devices in the first place.

But Cañon City parents were up in arms that their teens may actually be charged with a felony—the distribution of child pornography—as a result of sending these pictures. It's true that law enforcement is an awfully blunt instrument for dealing with these issues. But no one else seems to be taking this problem seriously.

In a piece for the *Atlantic* called "Why Kids Sext,"[35] Hanna Rosin tried to understand the motivation behind the behavior as well as what the consequences should be for the kids who engage in it. She tells the story of a fourteen-year-old girl named Jasmine whose nude picture wound up on Instagram, along with those of dozens of her fellow students. Jasmine was a straight-A student, who participated in sports, worked, and volunteered after school. But apparently she sent a naked picture to a boyfriend, or someone who wanted to be her boyfriend, and then he sent it to others. So did a number of other girls at her school. Her mother called the police.

From talking to the school's resource officer, Major Donald Lowe, Rosin concludes that most of the girls involved in this incident weren't particularly embarrassed by having their pictures up. And they weren't surprised either. Some girls had told the officer, "This is my life and my body and I can do whatever I want with it," or "I don't see any problem with it. I'm proud of my body." Some girls even tried to get their photos posted. Rosin writes, "In the first couple of weeks of the investigation, Lowe's characterization of the girls on Instagram morphed from 'victims" to 'I guess I'll call them victims' to 'they just fell into this category where they victimized themselves.'"

But what does it mean to say that a high school freshman whose nude photo is online for the world to see has victimized herself? Even if some of these kids claimed to have known what the consequences of their actions would be, how can they possibly understand what it means in the long term? And maybe we shouldn't take their word for it. Teenagers often like to act blasé about all sorts of things around adults even if they are actually upset about what's happened. It's true that arresting all the kids involved is probably not the ideal solution to a sexting ring. Or at any rate, it's too late. But law enforcement is simply acting where parents and educators have failed to.

In a similar case at Duxbury High School, in a suburb of Boston, authorities found pictures of fifty female students in "varying states of undress" in an online drop box. Police were trying to find the person who created the site, but it's not clear whether they will prosecute people who sent the pictures to the creator of the repository as well. As for the girls in the pictures, Duxbury's superintendent, Dr. Ben Tantillo, told the press, "We would hope that our young girls understand that there are other ways to be popular."[36]

It is easy to laugh at this comment, but Tantillo seems to understand that this is a problem whose solutions are cultural, not legal. Parents especially are going to be tasked with explaining to their children why the short-term gain of popularity or interest from a boy is not going to outweigh their long-term interests in college admissions, job opportunities, and serious romantic relationships.

But protecting kids from the effects of their online behavior goes beyond instructing them not to take these photos of themselves or send the ones they receive on to their friends. It also involves exerting a level of control over themselves at all times that may not have been necessary for previous generations. And for parents, it involves controlling access and closely monitoring kids' use of technology. How else is anything going to change?

In 2012, a fifteen-year-old girl named Audrie Potts committed suicide—the result, according to local reports, of cyberbullying. Potts found pictures of herself on social media where she was drunk, naked, and had permanent marker all over her body. She had been to a party with classmates from her suburban high school. The next morning she received a message from one of those boys: "Lol that sh-t gets around haha everyone knows mostly everything hahaah."[37]

Unfortunately, Potts's case is hardly unique. In the same year, pictures and a video surfaced of a sixteen-year-old girl who was clearly incapacitated being sexually assaulted by two football players in Steubenville, Ohio. While many young women are voluntarily sending out pictures of themselves in compromising positions, others are being photographed without their consent and even without their knowledge. The drinking culture in high school and college is a subject for another book, but it seems true that the number of kids (and particularly girls) who are drinking to the point of passing out has risen. (This is another area where grown-ups like to note that they too drank in high school so nothing has changed. But much has, in fact, changed.)

As a thought experiment, it would be worth it to fathom what it would have taken thirty years ago to achieve the same effect as what happened to these girls. Let's say you're a teenage boy and you actually got a girl alone and roaring drunk. Let's say you managed to get her to pass out and then you took off her clothes. And then it occurred to you that you wanted to commemorate the occasion.

You searched high and low for your camera. You took your picture and then brought in the film to CVS to be developed, at which point someone at CVS might have called the police. But let's say you had some Polaroids. Then you posted the results on bulletin boards all over your high school. Or did you use a mimeograph machine to distribute the photo? The whole process was much harder. Therefore, it was much less tempting and commonplace.

It is easy to understand why the kind of humiliation that resulted from these photos caused Potts to take her own life. This is simply a more extreme version of the kind of drama that goes on constantly in American high schools.

You might think there's nothing particularly shocking here—it's just teenagers being teenagers. And indeed some experts are putting data to use, calming parents' fears. A Pew report explains that "the digital realm is one part of a broader universe in which teens meet, date and break up with romantic partners." Social media is one piece of a puzzle: "Online spaces are used infrequently for meeting romantic partners, but play a major role in how teens flirt, woo and communicate with potential and current flames."[38]

All of that "wooing"—and not just the noodz—is different in many ways. Most importantly because of how incessant it is. According to the Pew survey, more than a third of teens in romantic relationships expect to hear from their partners every few hours and another 11 percent expect to hear from them every hour. As one thirteen-year-old told Nancy Jo Sales, "Probably more stuff happens on my phone than in real life."[39]

Teens are communicating more often thanks to social media—and they're also saying things they'd never dream of saying in person. According to the description of *#Being13* on CNN's website, "The level of profanity, explicit sexual language and references to drug use surprised the experts, considering the study's subjects were only in eighth grade."[40]

Social media doesn't change the teen years in any fundamental way. It just makes everything you remember about them much worse. Almost every parent of a teenager I spoke to told me that they had to help their children deal with the fear of missing out.

Parents are caught between wanting to make sure that their kids are not complete outcasts—that they know what's going on in school and have some ability to socialize with their classmates—while at the same time wanting to shield them from some of the harsh realities of teen drama.

Unfortunately, it seems that the dramas are getting harsher. And today we have to err more than ever on the side of shielding them. Which may mean not buying kids the gadgets they say will make them popular. It may mean that parents should be keeping their kids phone free for as long as possible. If adolescents and teens do get phones, they have to be monitored. This will not be easy. Neither Google nor YouTube nor any company that markets violent or sexual content has any financial interest in keeping it away from your kids. The same is true of social media. The more addictive it is, the more money they make.

It is time to ignore the reassurances of so-called parenting experts and well-compensated technophiles. We really have entered a brave new world. The content really is much more violent and much more sexually explicit. And the mistakes kids make online really are permanent and have the potential to damage their social lives, their education, their careers, and their emotional well-being. Adolescents have never been very good at looking out for their long-term interests. So now more than ever it is up to us.

We have to protect them from themselves, but not only from themselves. It's what parents used to say when their kids got behind the wheel of a car. Yes, we trust you—it's the other drivers we're not so sure about. When it comes to kids and technology, don't ask yourself if you trust your kids. Ask yourself if you trust their peers.

CHAPTER 6

# Think American Education Can't Get Worse? Put iPads in the Classroom

■ ■ ■ ■

IN 2000, I started traveling around the country to research a book on higher education. Over the course of a year and a half, I visited about two dozen colleges and observed more than a hundred courses. I wasn't there to study the way kids were using technology, but there were things I couldn't help but notice sitting in the back of a lecture hall. First, obviously, an increasing number of kids were bringing their laptops to class. Second, a whole lot of them were playing games on them. I remember watching one class in particular at a small college in Virginia. About half of the fifty students were using laptops, and almost without exception, all of those were playing solitaire and typing notes only occasionally, if at all.

This was before the days of Wi-Fi-equipped classrooms—so no communication or web surfing was even possible—but already students were tempted into using their technology for something besides listening to their professors. College kids have always zoned out during boring lectures—my father tells the story of a fellow graduate student who used to read the newspaper during class—but technology is clearly effecting how much we're taking in during school hours.

In a study released in 2016, economics professors at West Point found that students who used laptops in class performed worse than those who didn't. Susan Payne Carter, Kyle Greenberg, and Michael Walker divided students in an introductory economics class into three sections—those who could use computers freely in class, those who could use a tablet but only to look at course material, and those who were not allowed to use technology at all.[1]

The results, which were published by the School Effectiveness and Inequality Initiative at MIT, showed first of all that students who were only permitted to look at course material on devices (tablets had to be flat on the desk and visible to the professor at all times) actually used them 40 percent less than students in the classroom who were free to use technology.

Which makes sense. Whether they would admit it or not, many students are bringing laptops and tablets to class specifically because they want to be able to check Facebook, email their friends, or surf the web whenever they get bored with a lecture. Many adults do this too. If you walk into a meeting and everyone is on a laptop, do not anticipate a very engaged discussion.

The other important finding from the West Point experiment was that the use of technology hurt academic performance. On the final exam, students in the sections that allowed some form of device use scored 18 percent of a standard deviation lower than students in the section where devices were banned. Even those who were using the technology for specifically classroom purposes scored lower. According to the report: "By way of comparison, this effect is as large as the average difference in exam scores for two students whose cumulative GPAs [grade point averages] at the start of the semester differ by one-third of a standard deviation." Given that the exam counted for a quarter of the course grade, these differences could certainly mean the difference between passing and failing, the professors noted.

So what does it mean that the technology seemed to harm even the students who were using it for its intended academic purpose? For one thing, the report suggests, digital note taking simply may not be as effective as the old-fashioned kind. Indeed, there is plenty of evidence for this. A 2014 study by Pam Mueller of Princeton and Daniel Oppenheimer of University of California Los Angeles found that "even when laptops are used solely to take notes, they may still be impairing learning because their use results in shallower processing."[2]

Writing in the journal *Psychological Science*, the authors observed that "in three studies . . . students who took notes on laptops performed worse on conceptual questions than students who took notes longhand. We show that whereas taking more notes can be beneficial, laptop note takers' tendency to transcribe lectures verbatim rather than processing information and reframing it in their own words is detrimental to learning."[3]

Explaining the findings in *Scientific American*, columnist Cindi May suggests that this disparity may have something to do with the speed at which we take notes on a laptop compared with by hand:

> Writing by hand is slower and more cumbersome than typing, and students cannot possibly write down every word in a lecture. Instead, they listen, digest, and summarize so that they can succinctly capture the essence of the information. Thus, taking notes by hand forces the brain to engage in some heavy "mental lifting," and these efforts foster comprehension and retention. By contrast, when typing students can easily produce a written record of the lecture without processing its meaning, as faster typing speeds allow students to transcribe a lecture word for word without devoting much thought to the content.[4]

So what does all this mean for the parents of teenagers who are concerned about their children's education? By the time kids get to middle school and high school, it is easy for parents to leave decisions about technology in the classroom up to the teachers and administrators. The question of whether a teacher or a school allows, encourages, or even provides technology for our kids seems like one best left to the experts. Ironically, though, one of the biggest reasons that schools are using technology is to impress parents.

*Tips for Cutting Back*

Question everything. If your child's school seems to be pouring technology into the classroom, ask why. Find out exactly what assignments require the use of a computer and which ones students have the option of doing the old-fashioned way. Ask administrators for evidence that the technology is improving learning outcomes.

Lowell Monke, a former computer science teacher at a public high school before going on to be a professor at Wittenberg University, says he actually thinks most parents are more careful about giving kids technology than professional educators are: "I was amazed at how much more thoughtlessly schools were willing to adopt this stuff than parents." Monke believes that this unthinking adoption of technology is "all about schools being scared to death that they are going to get criticized for not having the latest and greatest tools for the kids."

Todd Bucholz, a former White House economic policy adviser who has his own classroom software company, says it is "easier to demonstrate computer programs on parent teacher night." He believes that in particular "private schools are in a kind of arms race as schools brag about what they have in terms of technology." But the truth is that public schools are competing, too. The wealthy districts want to show what they are offering kids in return for outrageous property taxes. The low-income districts, meanwhile, want to show that they are doing everything they can to improve school quality. And the easiest way to demonstrate all of this is to buy a bunch of stuff for classrooms.

Bucholz says, "I have been concerned that there have been purchases of technology without looking at whether what you put on it is good." He estimates, for instance, that "80–90 percent of math games for elementary school kids seem to be drilling. You might as well do it with flash cards. Just because there's a rocket ship next to your addition problem doesn't mean you will learn it better."

Unfortunately, like a parent who demonstrates affection by purchasing his or her child a lot of expensive toys for Christmas, the advent of new technology in schools does not necessarily improve education, and it certainly doesn't say anything about the long-term commitment of these schools to help students.

A 2016 article in the *Wall Street Journal* called "Look Mom, I'm Writing a Term Paper on My Cellphone" quoted one teacher in New York City, New York, who encourages kids to do projects on their phones. "If you want to become a disruptive teacher in 2016, you have to figure out how to log on with [students] and explain to them in their community," she says. "If you don't embrace the fact that they are always logged on, you are not going to reach them in the way they're comfortable."[5]

The students are creating PowerPoint presentations on their phones as well as using Google Docs to share their essays. Students are even using their phones to take quizzes so teachers can get a quick sense of whether students have understood the lesson. Which all sounds great. But the question is whether these benefits outweigh the phone's potential for distraction. And the answer is clearly no.

"The phone could be a great equalizer, in terms of giving children from all sorts of socioeconomic backgrounds the same devices, with the same advantages," writes Paul Barnwell, an English teacher in Louisville, Kentucky, in an essay for the *Atlantic*. "But using phones for learning requires students to synthesize information and stay focused on a lesson or a discussion. For students with low literacy skills and the frequent urge to multitask on social media or entertainment, incorporating purposeful smartphone use into classroom activity can be especially challenging."[6] A study by the London School of Economics found that "banning mobile phones improves outcomes for the low-achieving students . . . the most, and has no significant impact on high achievers."[7]

A similar dynamic has played out with technology used by children in the home. A 2010 National Bureau of Economic Research study found that "the introduction of home computer technology is associated with modest but statistically significant and persistent negative impacts on student math and reading test scores."[8] Examining data for 150,000 students between 2000 and 2005, the authors found that technology is put to productive use in the homes of more well-off children because parents are monitoring it, but it is a distraction to children in lower-income homes where parents are often not monitoring it. The researchers conclude that "providing universal access to home computers and high-speed internet access would broaden, rather than narrow, math and reading achievement gaps."

. . . .

Politicians and educators regularly talk about technology as the way to solve educational and income inequality in our country. Most schools that cater to low-income children are trying to get them more technology, not less. Schools show parents these shiny new toys as evidence that they are giving their children a leg up, helping to bridge the so-called digital divide. What is more likely is that too much access to technology is actually exacerbating the inequality that already exists.

Take the incidences of ADHD. Researchers Paul L. Morgan of Pennsylvania State University and George Farkas of University of California Irvine have found that though they are often underdiagnosed, black children are more likely to show symptoms of ADHD than their white peers.[9] While the authors cite factors such as elevated lead levels in the blood of children in poorer neighborhoods and environmental factors including widespread poverty and single-parent households that they find are correlated with learning disabilities, Morgan and Farkas seem to overlook a potentially large reason why minority children are more likely to be displaying attention problems disproportionately.

According to a 2011 study by researchers at Northwestern University, minority kids watch 50 percent more television than their white peers. Daily, they use computers for up to one-and-a-half hours longer and play video games for thirty to forty minutes longer than their white peers. There are statistically significant differences in the number of hours that white and minority kids spend on screens per day.[10] According to Kaiser, white children spend eight hours, thirty-six minutes in front of a screen per day compared to black and Hispanic kids at thirteen hours. And children of parents with a college degree consume about an hour and a half less per day than kids with less-educated parents.[11]

Giving kids more access to screens is clearly not the answer to the education gap in this country. And yet when New York Mayor Bill de Blasio announced plans to build one of the largest municipal Wi-Fi networks in the world, delivering Internet access to poorer areas, he said it would be "bridging the digital divide."[12]

In 2014, New York received a half-million dollar grant to loan Internet hotspots to families who can't afford access at home. According to the Urban Libraries Council, such lending programs are "the latest buzz." Similar programs have launched in Chicago, Seattle, and St. Paul, Minnesota, with funding coming from Google, among other companies. As the council explains, "With the movement to mobile learning becoming more prevalent in schools, closing the digital literacy divide is becoming imperative."[13]

Perhaps it was inevitable that libraries, having become somewhat lost regarding their purpose in the modern era of Internet research and Amazon Prime, have settled on the crusade against the digital divide. But it is a shame, particularly for less-advantaged kids, who still need adults to teach them how to read well and how to enjoy reading.

Instead, the result is a lot of flashiness but not a lot of places for deep reading and learning. For instance, the recent renovations to the White Plains Library in the suburbs of New York included "a social area with a big-screen television for gaming and movies; a mixing area with computer workstations and study areas; and a media lab for teens to learn how to use digital media equipment and work on projects." The library's director, Brian Kenney, explained to the local paper,

"As a library we should be sure we're creating experiences that will attract our users. And teens, we know, are interested in digital content."[14]

There's no doubt Kenney will pat himself on the back when he finds that the people making use of these digital experiences are from lower-income backgrounds. But he should know that their wealthier peers, meanwhile, will likely be skipping screen time at the library. Their parents will be keeping them at home—reading books.

Less-educated and lower-income parents also typically see media as less of a threat to their children. According to a Pew survey, "Parents living in low-income households (earning less than $30,000 per year) express significantly lower levels of concern about their children's online interactions with people they do not know; just 39% say they are 'very concerned' about this issue, compared with about six in ten parents in higher-earning households."[15]

■ ■ ■

Research on digital devices is not as extensive as it was for television and video games, but we have been trying to use computers to improve education for some time now. Larry Cuban, Stanford University education professor, has been looking at the question of technology in the classroom for three decades. He tells me, "I can say pretty categorically that there is no evidence that use of devices and software will improve academic achievement of students."

In his book *Inside the Black Box of Classroom Practice*, Cuban attributes two factors to the hype for technology despite its poor results to two factors. "First," he tells me, "there is the novelty effect to explain student engagement with high-tech. New devices—think clickers in an algebra class or iPads for kindergartners—motivate students initially, but as time passes, the effects wear off. Second, major studies have repeatedly shown weak to no linkage between these devices or software and substantial changes in teaching practices or improved test scores." The decisions about classroom technology are generally made by school boards and superintendents—without much input from teachers, says Cuban. But teachers are the ones who are going to have to integrate the technology into their classrooms.

In other words, technology is not permanently changing the things—teaching styles and student excitement—that would improve student achievement. But there is plenty of evidence that abundant technology is making the classroom environment worse.

In his recent book *Substitute,* novelist Nicholson Baker gives an account of twenty-eight days he spent filling in for teachers at elementary, middle, and high schools in Maine.[16] Perhaps the most significant difference between the classrooms that Baker describes and the ones that most adults remember is the presence of technology. Since 2011, Maine has had a "one-to-one program"—one iPad for each student.

When Baker is substituting, his instructions usually involve having the kids complete an assignment on their devices. After each set of instructions, there is a chorus of announcements from students: The Internet connection is not working. They can't understand how to make a program operate. Their access has been restricted.

The entire system seems designed to drive teachers insane and prevent students from learning. Kids are on their iPads doing things unrelated to their schoolwork—playing games and listening to music—or even using iPad cases to beat each other over the head. Some are even looking at "inappropriate material" in the back of the classroom. And unless a teacher is standing over students, the teacher won't be able to tell who is actually doing the work and who is playing games. Even when the devices are used for educational purposes, they are undermining teachers rather than helping them. Teachers ask for the definition of words and students just look them up online and give the answers verbatim rather than actually thinking about the question and seeing if they can come up with an answer on their own.

On one level, parents know this. We know what happens when we give our kids screens. We know that the second they turn on the iPad or take out the phone, they will have a hard time listening to anything we say. The effects in a classroom are not much different.

So why do we think they will be? For one thing, there are forces out there that pressure us to believe that time on a screen will make our children smarter and more capable adults. Those forces start, most obviously, with the producers of the technology. As Cuban notes, there are "vendors constantly putting pressure on us because of the market." In the world of educational technology, "public schools spend hundreds of billions of dollars. Whenever there is a market in this capitalistic democratic society, there will be external pressure for schools to buy technology." Cuban calls it "pervasive and unrelenting."

It is useful to remember that school boards are political institutions. They are dependent on the financial and political support from parents and communities. By the time technology was introduced in schools in the early 1980s, a lot of other industries in the country had been transformed by it. But the real pressure to bring in technology to the classroom began in the 1990s, says Cuban, when American students were compared to others on international tests and found to be lacking. The jobs that were out there were much more information based and so "all of the pressure came down on schools." More and more school districts introduced one-to-one programs for devices. "They want to keep up with the Joneses," says Cuban.

When I ask Heather Kirkorian whether parents need to give their kids devices at a young age so they won't be left behind, she tells me, "I don't think there is a cause for concern about being prepared." Indeed, there is no evidence that screen-free classrooms or home environments where kids are not given screens until later will somehow fall behind. "Young kids pick things up quickly," she notes. "I don't think it's realistic to say their kids won't be successful if they are not learning on a tablet or computer."

But the pressures to give our kids time with technology are not simply coming from tech companies or from schools. They are coming from other families. It is hard to be in a community where everyone has a phone or an iPad and your kid does not. It is inconvenient for other parents in carpools or kids' friends who want to make social plans for the weekend. In a few short years, our worlds have completely shifted—the assumption now is that everyone over the age of eleven has a mobile device. And that number is getting younger and younger.

Some parents do wonder whether and when to hand over the devices, but they are met with surprising reassurance from the experts. Indeed, there is no shortage of authors who are willing to advise parents about how and when they should use technology with their kids. Take Rosalind Wiseman, whose blockbuster book *Queen Bees and Wannabes* formed the basis for the 2004 hit movie *Mean Girls*. She tells me that thanks to the ubiquity of devices and the reach of social media, "the scope of the damage girls can do is wider. And there are fewer brakes on their behavior."

In the third edition of her book, Wiseman adds an extensive section on technology, in which she offers a few basic rules for limiting its use. She says devices shouldn't be used at the dinner table. They distract from connecting with family. They probably shouldn't be in kids' rooms at night because they distract from sleeping. And she tells me that she advises parents to collect phones before sleepover parties because "someone is going to send a picture of themselves naked to someone else."

Given all these ill effects, it's rather surprising that Wiseman doesn't suggest parents seriously curtail their kids' use of technology or refrain from buying them smartphones in the first place. She says no one asks her at what age they should get their kids a phone anymore, and she doesn't have any suggestions. Like many parents and other experts she cites, including technophile and Microsoft researcher danah boyd, Wiseman sees this as a losing battle: "No matter what experts or the hypervigilant parent in your neighborhood tells you, it's actually really hard to know everything your child is doing all the time online."[17]

No doubt this is true, but the fact is that more and more of those experts have decided to throw their hands up. Some like Wiseman will tell you that the technology is really too hard to control. Others will tell you that technology has the potential to help your kids academically. Some will tell you it's just a matter of using the right apps or installing the right filters. Still others will warn that if kids don't have enough access now, they'll go crazy with it when they're older.

. . . .

Unfortunately, there seems to be a dangerous convergence here between parents who want their kids to have the latest tools and the booming educational technology sector, which is trying to get software, hardware, curricula, and classroom management systems into every school in America.

According to a report from the Education Technology Industry Network, the educational technology market totaled $8.38 billion in the 2012–13 academic year. That number is up from $7.9 billion the year before and 11.7 percent from 2009.[18] And investors have taken note of the tremendous growth, not only in course materials that are provided to students but also in assessment tools.

According to *EdSurge*, these companies raised $1.36 billion in 2014, up from $1.2 billion in 2013. For the elementary and secondary school market alone, investment grew 32 percent in 2014 to $642 million.[19] For decades, the companies trying to get into classrooms were textbook publishers. Parents, teachers, and school boards were involved in bitter battles over the content of the textbooks as well as the costs. How often could school districts purchase new versions of the old textbooks? How often should they?

In 2013, the Los Angeles Unified Public School District began handing out iPads as part of a $1.3 billion digital learning program. By 2015, it had become clear that the program had failed, and the FBI started investigating the preferential treatment that both Apple and Pearson (a curriculum company) received from district administrators in the process. Michael Horn, executive director of the education program at the Christensen Institute, told *Wired* magazine that the Los Angeles fiasco is a case of a school district getting caught up in the educational technology frenzy. "A lot of schools get into trouble when the conversation starts with the vendor," Horn says.[20] In other words, what schools know is that they want to buy something. But they are not clear on what they want the technology to do for their kids.

It is only recently that parents have begun to understand the deal that their schools and their district representatives have struck with education technology companies, often without enough evidence to make these purchases worthwhile. Tony Wan, the managing editor of *EdSurge*, told the *Atlantic* that in the past, schools initiated a lengthy "request for proposal" process and looked at products from a variety of different companies—a process that could take as long as two years, which is "a lifetime for most startups."[21] Now, schools are allowing companies to come into classrooms to demonstrate their products right away. Which means schools can show parents the cutting-edge stuff they're doing with students and parents can walk away thinking that their kid is getting a better education.

But it's not just that these companies are making money off of these schools now. Silicon Valley is also trying to shape the future of education. As a recent series in the *New York Times* noted, "In the space of just a few years, technology giants have begun remaking the very nature of schooling on a vast scale, using some of the same techniques that have made their companies linchpins of the American economy. Through their philanthropy, they are influencing the subjects that schools teach, the classroom tools that teachers choose, and fundamental approaches to learning."[22]

Facebook's Mark Zuckerberg and his wife are promoting personalized online learning at more than one hundred schools. A nonprofit organization called Code.org, which counts Microsoft among its funders, "has barnstormed the country, pushing states to change education laws and fund computer science courses. It has also helped more than 120 districts to introduce such curriculums, the group said, and has facilitated training workshops for more than 57,000 teachers."[23] While there's no doubt that learning computer code is a marketable skill, it remains an open question whether teaching it to elementary school children is the best use of their time and a school's resources.

But many schools are invested much more heavily into learning with technology. Take online recovery credit, in which students take courses online that they failed in a classroom. In 2016, the *Atlanta Journal Constitution* reported that "Georgia students took more than 20,700 online 'credit recovery' courses last year. . . . About 90 percent of Georgia students who took one of these courses last year in subjects covered by state tests passed the course itself. But an *Atlanta Journal-Constitution* analysis of results of the state-required tests found only about 10 percent of them were proficient in the subject."[24]

An eight-part series on the website *Slate* looked into the question of online credit recovery and found that while many districts and states had improved their graduation rates, there was little evidence that students were grasping the material being offered in these screen-based classes. Because these courses vary to such a degree, the National Collegiate Athletic Association (NCAA) "now contacts school districts to gauge how much time online courses take to complete and how much interaction students have with instructors. The vast majority fails to pass muster, according to Nick Sproull, whose high school review department oversees inspection efforts for the NCAA."[25]

One of the only things to be said with certainty about educational technology is that it is good at evaluating kids. Students who get math problems wrong will be offered new ones that are specifically geared toward helping determine which concept they are missing. Students who are reading on screens may be able to look up words that they do not understand, thereby sending an alert to a teacher who can add them to the week's vocabulary quiz.

If used correctly, educational technology can help teachers understand exactly what kids are not getting. Sometimes this is done formally. I was in a classroom a few years ago when a physics teacher took a break from his lecture to ask students a multiple choice question. Each was armed with a clicker, and instantly the professor could tell by the tally on his own computer how many kids were following what he was saying. Only about half had gotten the answer correctly, so he went back and tried to explain the concept again. Not only is this way of conducting a class more exact than simply asking students as a whole whether they understand, it is also less embarrassing for those who are falling behind.

Technology can also be used to help administrators and school leaders understand more about their staffs. The use of teacher evaluations in determining compensation and promotion has been quite controversial, but what technology can offer is a regular sense of what is going on in a classroom. Rather than just relying on standardized test scores once a year, administrators and teachers themselves can figure out what they are doing right and wrong. The teachers who have been more successful at getting kids to understand a particular topic could, in principle, share their secrets.

One of the major selling points of educational technology is that it could personalize learning to an unprecedented degree. Ted Kolderie, a longtime education prognosticator, has noted that much of what is missing from our conversation about fixing American schools has been the question of how to "motivate" our students.[26] Because educational technology ideally allows students to move at their own pace, motivation can come much easier for them.

Here are some questions parents should keep in mind when trying to evaluate whether their schools are using technology simply because the new tools seem cool or because they genuinely have the chance of improving learning outcomes. Are the things that are appearing on students' screens simply fancy flash cards? Are students working on things at a different pace than their classmates? How do teachers explain the use of these devices and this software? How were these educational technology companies picked? Did they simply go right to the classroom or is there evidence of their products' effectiveness?

It's important to keep in mind that some of the most effective innovations in educational technology are not ones that seem slick or entertaining. Khan Academy videos explaining math concepts are not filled with flashing lights or exciting graphics but they have been viewed millions of times by students who need clear explanations for complex concepts.

There are plenty of other possibilities as well for individualizing student learning through technology and for improving education as a whole. Amplify, a company that offers digital and print curricula in more than sixty school districts, uses multimedia platforms to improve kids' learning experience. When students are studying Frederick Douglass, for instance, they can watch actor Chadwick Boseman recite six pages of Douglass's autobiography. They can play games on an iPad that allow them to explore the topics of classic books and find more books they might like to read.

One of Amplify's most successful ventures is a game called *Twelve a Dozen* (which is also now available for purchase by anyone). A little character called "12" wanders through a Mario Bros.–looking landscape, but he can only go over bridges or jump over lakes or lift blocks if he turns himself into another number (using different math functions). Kids have to figure out the right order to accomplish these functions, and the game always lets players rewind to where they think they made a mistake and try it again. I don't know if the game is enough "fun" to draw in kids who might otherwise not like or be intimidated by math, but it certainly seems to stretch the minds of those who are. And I'd have a hard time thinking of the flash card equivalent.

Larry Berger, the chief executive officer of Amplify, says he takes a different approach to technology than some other digital learning companies. "I think my starting point is: what are the things that technology can do as a tool of attention rather than an attention disruptor?" That's one reason the company does not have kids working on digital devices before sixth grade. And Amplify's programs do not often utilize screens like regular adult computers. The screens that the kids use for reading are not backlit in the same way. There are relatively few hyperlinks in the text, and they can be turned off completely. In other words, Amplify eliminates a lot of the distractions.

Limiting the distractions for students is likely a good idea, considering few adults can manage them. Just like every other aspect of parenting, the approach to technology for students needs to take into account the fact that these kids aren't adults. And there is much we want them to learn before we send them out into the world on their own.

Like what is the purpose of technology in our lives? When our kids look at us, they see it is our lifeline, allowing us to work from home and go to soccer games to watch our kids while also ensuring that we can never quite disconnect from the office to pay total attention to our families and friends. Kids can start to see how their laptops provide a dual purpose: they can write papers and do problem sets as well as be entertained and connect constantly to their friends. But what they probably won't recognize is how hard it is to pay attention when technology is ubiquitous.

## *Tips for Cutting Back*

Don't answer right away. When kids ask for a new app, a new device, or new content, do not answer on the spot. Do your homework. Figure out exactly what this access will mean for them. Use a site like Common Sense Media to figure out exactly what's age appropriate.

New technology is referred to as a "disruptor." This term is used often to describe how a novel device or program changes the business landscape. Uber was a disruptor for the taxicab industry. Amazon was a disruptor for booksellers. As consumers, we see the positive connotations of these changes. But technology has also become a disruptor for families, disrupting our conversations, our dinners, our trip to the zoo. And it is disrupting the way our children pursue their goals, both in school and out of it.

In her 2016 book, *Grit: The Power of Passion and Perseverance*, Angela Duckworth writes: "In the long run, culture has the power to shape our identity. Over time and under the right circumstances, the norms and values of the group to which we belong become our own."[27] Those values can help us to engage in the kind of perseverance in the face of adversity that is vital to achieving difficult, long-term goals. But what about if cultural influences are the forces coming out of twenty-first-century America?

More and more, we live in a world of constant distraction,

which can prevent us from devoting the time and the focus to mastering a skill. Obviously, a lot of the problem comes from our devices. Looking at the questions that Duckworth uses to measure how gritty someone is—that is, how likely the person is to work at a goal and succeed over the long term in spite of obstacles—it is easy to see why constant interruptions would affect the score. In her book, respondents were asked to rate themselves on measures including "new ideas and projects sometimes distract me from previous ones" and "I have difficulty maintaining my focus on projects that take more than a few months to complete."

It's not just the distractions. It's how much less difficult the technological alternatives are when compared with pursuing other activities. If your choice is between playing a video game and reading a book, between swimming laps for hours and watching television, between texting your friends and practicing the violin, the answers are pretty simple for most kids.

In her review of *Grit* in the *New York Times*,[28] Judith Shulevitz notes that her immigrant grandfather would have instinctively understood Duckworth's message that talent matters, but effort matters more. No doubt there is an immigrant culture that can help to promote grit. (Duckworth writes about some of the children of immigrants who make it to the National Spelling Bee.) But one wonders whether grit was simply easier for previous generations to achieve.

We cannot turn back the clock. It is up to us, then, to teach our kids how to shut out some of those distractions. We can still make them go to swim practice or pick up the violin and turn off the television. Unfortunately, many schools have simply given up trying to restrict technology-based distractions and instead have welcomed them with open arms.

In the last chapter, I described the pornographic text message that writer Amy Anderson received (on behalf of her son), but I left out what might have been the most revealing part:

> Looking at when the image had been delivered, I figured my son had been in math class at the time at his Catholic high school. And given that the school had done away with books in favor of an "innovative" all-digital classroom, he must have received the naked shot instantly. (School administrators: stop kidding yourself. Unless the teen students are using devices that don't allow Internet access, chances are they're not listening to the lecture on *Macbeth* but watching Netflix or, worse, Pornhub.)[29]

Study after study has shown that people read much less and comprehend much less when they are looking at a web page than when they are reading a book. A 2005 study called "Reading Behavior in the Digital Environment" in the *Journal of Documentation* found that "the screen-based reading behavior is characterized by more time spent on browsing and scanning, keyword spotting, one-time reading, non-linear reading, and reading more selectively, while less time is spent on in-depth reading, and concentrated reading. Decreasing sustained attention is also noted."[30]

These are effects that we all feel intuitively. In his book, *The Shallows*, Nicholas Carr describes the change he could feel his brain experiencing around 2005 when social media began to take over:

> I began to notice that the Net was exerting a much stronger and broader influence over me than my old stand-alone PC ever had. . . . It was then that I began worrying about my inability to pay atten-

tion to one thing for more than a couple of minutes. . . . My brain, I realized, wasn't just drifting. It
was hungry. It was demanding to be fed the way the
Net fed it—and the more it was fed, the hungrier
it became. Even when I was away from my computer, I yearned to check email, click links, do some
Googling. I wanted to be connected.[31]

Here is Carr, a professional writer and an adult with
decades of experience concentrating on books finding it hard
to concentrate. How do we expect high school kids to do it?
Daniel Self, a sixteen-year-old North Carolina student who
uses his cell phone for classwork, told the *Wall Street Journal*:
"When someone texts you, tags you on Instagram, you see all
that stuff and it's really tempting," he said. "But most of the
time I know I have to finish my work in a reasonable manner,
and it's all about self-control."[32]

At what age do kids have this kind of self-control? Most
adults barely have it. A 2016 article in the *New York Times*
described the importance of "monotasking." The ability to
focus on a single thing is "a digital literacy skill," says Manoush
Zomorodi, the host and managing editor of the *Note to Self*
podcast on WNYC.[33] Kelly McGonigal, a psychologist and
the author of *The Willpower Instinct*, believes that focusing
on one thing is "something that needs to be practiced." She
says: "It's an important ability and a form of self-awareness
as opposed to a cognitive limitation."[34] McGonigal and others
have found that engaging in multitasking makes it more likely
that people will make errors and also less likely that they will
actually enjoy what they are doing. But try telling that to a
high school student in a history class with a phone buzzing in
his pocket. If you want your children to practice monotasking,
you're going to have to make them do it themselves. Because

the likelihood is that their school will be pushing them in the opposite direction.

In his book *Amusing Ourselves to Death*, Neal Postman observes that "education [today] is indistinguishable from entertainment."[35] And how could it be otherwise? Our teachers now feel that they have to use every shiny gadget they encounter in their classroom or their students will simply be bored. They are used to fast-paced and sometimes graphic video games, sexually explicit material, and the constant feedback loop of social media. What attraction could reading and analyzing a novel possibly hold for them?

In the very moments when we want our children to be engaged with each other and to be thinking deeply about the material in front of them, they are checking to see whether their friends are doing something more interesting, whether someone has liked their selfie, or whether there is a racy photo of their classmate that has gone viral. We are allowing them to keep on their desks or in their backpacks some of the biggest obstacles to sustained thought.

In the 1970s, researchers undertook a study in Canada, comparing children in three remote towns. Due to geographic factors, two of the towns got television before the third. Researchers looked at the third town, Notel, just before television was introduced in 1973 and two years afterward. The findings were dramatic. Before the introduction of television, kids in Notel scored higher on various measures, including levels of creativity and reading ability. After the advent of television, there was no difference.[36]

Other studies have shown a strong correlation between watching an excessive amount of television or other screens and lower academic performance, but the Notel study shows that the arrival of television actually caused the same students in the same schools with the same teachers and the same families to score lower on tests after a mere two years.

Rather than assuming that television somehow undermined kids' capabilities, the researchers suggested that it was actually the amount of time kids were spending in front of the screen that had altered their academic performance. More time on television meant less time reading or engaging in imaginary play—or sleeping for that matter.

But time on screens also has affected the actual quality of the reading experience. Looking at websites and reading Facebook posts, tweets, or Instagram photos all day has made sustained reading more difficult for all of us. Carr notes that "while a page of online text viewed through a computer screen may seem similar to a page of printed text," they are quite different. "Reading a book was a meditative act, but it didn't involve a clearing of the mind. It involved a filling, or replenishing, of the mind. Readers disengaged their attention from the outward flow of passing stimuli in order to engage it more deeply with an inward flow of words, ideas and emotions."[37] This is not what typically happens when we read a web page. Whatever the reason, multiple experiments have shown that readers simply do not gain the same level of comprehension reading on a screen that they do on paper.

Indeed, kids may not immerse themselves in books the same way when they are reading on a screen. A couple of years ago, I bought my daughter a Kindle. The screen wasn't backlit. There were no pop-up ads or hyperlinks. It was as close to reading a book as you could get without the paper. After begging for it for months, she never seemed quite as comfortable with it as she did with a book. Other mothers have reported the same experience. The Kindle gathers dust while more and more paperbacks are purchased.

With books, my daughter curled up. She bent their pages to keep her place, took them with her in the car, to a beach, on the school bus. The books came back beat up, wrinkled, wet, but she took deep satisfaction in finishing them and placing each one on the shelf next to the rest of her library. When our kids are reading on tablets, by contrast, we admonish them not to lose the device, to be careful how they touch it, to remember where they put it, to not drop it, and so on. But books are different. Kids experience the feel of them.

It is hard to lose yourself as completely in an e-book. This may be one reason that despite the predictions of pundits about the end of print books, electronic book sales are stagnant or diminishing. According to a 2013 Pew report, the percentage of adults who have read an e-book rose from 2012 to 2013. But it also stated that 89 percent of regular book readers said that they had read at least one printed book during the preceding year. Only 30 percent reported reading a single e-book.[38]

For adults, whose reading habits are already mostly formed, this may not be surprising. But what about kids? Do we want them to become more interested in e-books because these are the wave of the future? Or is it because we want them to be more comfortable with the technology? Or should we be more concerned with developing their relationship to reading?

Reading on a screen is harder in some ways. But it is the use of hypertext, which was supposed to give us a greater understanding of what we're reading, that has created one of the biggest problems. In one experiment, for example, Canadian scholars had seventy people read a short story and then asked them questions about what they had read. Those who read a text with hyperlinks reported more confusion and uncertainty. One even complained that the story was "jumpy." Keep in mind that not all experiments show

that reading with hypertext lowers a reader's level of comprehension.[39] But in 2007, psychologists Diana DeStefano and
Jo-Anne LeFevre reviewed thirty-eight previous experiments
and found, on the whole, that "the increased demands of
decision-making and visual processing in hypertext impaired
reading performance."[40]

So what happens when we send our kids to their rooms with
laptops and iPads to do reading or compose term papers? It
is not just that they may be spending time on apps that have
little to do with schoolwork. It is that they are being distracted
by the very reading they are supposed to be doing.

Even the websites of reputable sources—major newspapers
and prominent magazines—are chopping up content into
small bits so that people can digest them more easily. Edi-
tors and writers are inserting as many hyperlinks as possible.
There is a financial incentive to do so, after all. The more links
you get readers to click, the more money you can make. And
newspapers can use every penny these days.

But surely there must be an upside to the use of technology
when it comes to our kids' schoolwork. Parents who remember using flash cards to memorize historical dates or math-
ematical formulas may think that the use of computers and
tablets will allow kids to do less rote memorization and more
critical thinking. Hardly a day goes by when an educator does
not lecture parents on how kids don't need to learn facts now
because those are all available at the touch of a button. Why
would you memorize dates and names and places when one
could look them up so quickly? Why waste the space in your
brain?

The idea that the brain has a limited amount of capacity
and you should save it for important things is not a recent
notion. I remember my father used to tell me that Sherlock
Holmes said something similar. I recently went and looked it

up and sure enough, in a story called "A Study in Scarlet," Holmes tells Watson:

> I consider that a man's brain originally is like a little empty attic, and you have to stock it with such furniture as you choose. A fool takes in all the lumber of every sort that he comes across, so that the knowledge which might be useful to him gets crowded out, or at best is jumbled up with a lot of other things, so that he has a difficulty in laying his hands upon it.[41]

Modern science (not to mention personal experience) has shown this brain-attic theory to be nonsense. Most of us know very smart, capable people who also happen to have a lot of trivial information stored in their brains. When I think of friends who have clerked at the Supreme Court, I have found that their extensive knowledge of baseball records and Cole Porter lyrics have not gotten in the way of their ability to recite from historically significant majority opinions. Even my father mixes quotes from famous political philosophers with cereal jingles from his childhood.

In his book *The Overflowing Brain: Information Overload and the Limits of Working Memory*, Torkel Klingberg writes that "the amount of information that can be stored in long-term memory is virtually boundless."[42] There is also an amazing inefficiency to letting our computers store all the facts. If you have to write anything for a living—reports, books, memos, letters—you will find that it helps to have certain things memorized. College students who have to look up every fact online will quickly find themselves sucked into *Wikipedia* and unlikely to make much progress on a term paper.

As Carr writes, "We don't constrain our mental powers when we store new long-term memories. We strengthen them.

With each expansion of our memory comes an enlargement of our intelligence." He notes, "The Web provides a convenient and compelling supplement to personal memory, but when we start using the Web as a substitute for personal memory, bypassing the inner processes of consolidation, we risk emptying our minds of their riches."[43]

This emptying of the mind has not only resulted in a decline in academic performance in the United States, it has also hurt our children's desire to read outside of school too. The second might, of course, be a cause of the first. According to a 2015 survey conducted by YouGov on behalf of Scholastic Books, "only 51 percent of children said they love or like reading books for fun, compared to 58 percent in 2012, and 60 percent in 2010."[44] And there has been a steady decline for some time now. Per a survey done by the National Endowment for the Arts Between 1982 and 2002, there was a seventeen-point drop in the percentage of eighteen- to twenty-four-year-olds who read for pleasure.[45]

And older kids are less likely to read for pleasure than younger ones. According to Scholastic, 62 percent of children between six and eight say they either love or like reading books for fun, but only 46 percent of children between the ages of nine and eleven say the same. As kids approach adulthood, the number never gets above 50 percent.[46] Which is weird when you think about it. It should be that as reading becomes easier, as we become capable of reading longer, more involved stories, we should be enjoying it more. But that's not the case.

This decline may be easily tied to technology. Three-quarters of the parents surveyed by Scholastic said they wished their child would read more books for fun, and 71 percent said "I wish my child would do more things that did not involve screen time."[47]

As kids get older, there are more things to distract them from reading for pleasure. Many of those things are out of the control of parents, at least to some extent. Kids are in school for long hours and engaged in extracurricular activities on multiple afternoons a week. On the weekends, families are often on the go, trying to run all the errands there were no time for during the week. But for parents to say they wished their children would do more things that did not involve screens implies that parents can't control this aspect of their children's lives. Sure their lives are busy, but when you think about all the times that they spend waiting—in a doctor's office, in the car, on a bus, at a restaurant—there must be times they could be encouraged to read a book. Instead, we give them devices to make the time go by.

### Tips for Cutting Back

Books: don't leave home without them. You never know when a trip to the pharmacy is going to turn into something longer. If your children can read, make sure they always have a book on them. Even if they can't read yet, make sure there is something else for them to do in the car—Rubik's cube, coloring, dolls. Even scissors and tape can be handy for a quick art project.

Screens not only take away time from reading, they make reading harder and less satisfying because there are always other things that seem easier. Writing in *The Dumbest Generation*, Mark Bauerlein decries the fact that without guidance from adults—indeed sometimes with their encouragement—young people are wasting hours "in an online youth world, running up opportunity costs every time they check their MySpace page and neglect their English homework, paying for them years later when they can't read or write well enough to do academic work or qualify for a job, or know enough to answer simple questions about the scientific method, Rembrandt or Auschwitz."[48]

But it is not just some highfalutin standard to which Bauerlein, an English professor at Emory, is holding young adults. Corporate America spends billions each year on in-house literacy. And colleges spend billions on remedial education.

Middle-class American parents rightly spend a lot of time worrying about whether their kids will get a good education, whether they'll get into a good college, and whether they'll succeed afterward. But the onus cannot be entirely on the schools. The truth is that without adult supervision, teenagers will do what's easiest. And being online is easy. Selfies are easy. Snapchat is easy. Twitter is easy. Blogging is easy. Chronicling your own life, your feelings, the drama of your friends is easy.

But these are not the things that prepare you for adult life, at least not the kind of adult life that most of us want for our children. When one becomes used to reading the social media posts of friends, spending only a few seconds skimming through text or looking at pictures, other more important things will start to seem boring. After all this, Bauerlein wonders: "Who can endure an hours-long school board meeting? Why spend weeks listening to candidates and sorting out the issues then standing in line for two hours to vote . . . ?"[49]

When we are trying to determine what kind of people we'd like our kids to become, we must fully engage with the question of how we want them to be educated. It's not just that we want them to do well on the SATs or to put hours in each night on their homework so that they can get into a good college. It's also that we would like them to enjoy learning, to become curious or even passionate about at least one subject. The use of technology at school and at home is making this much harder.

It's time to stop sugarcoating the truth. The more we know, the better equipped we can be to push back against the pressures coming at us from all directions. And if these experts can't be depended upon to help us in this fight, well, so be it. We parents will have to simply do what we've been doing for a long time. Put our foot down. Power to the parents.

## CHAPTER 7

# Just Say No

■ ■ ■ ■

IN A 2016 ARTICLE in the *Atlantic*, Caitlin Flanagan asks: "Are you a Good Parent or a Get-Real Parent?" She describes them as: "Good Parents think that alcohol is dangerous for young people and that riotous drunkenness and its various consequences have nothing to recommend them. These parents enforce the law and create a family culture that supports their beliefs. Get-Real Parents think that high-school kids have been drinking since Jesus left Chicago, and that it's folly to pretend the new generation won't as well."[1] When it comes to technology, there is even more pressure to be a get-real parent. But just as with drinking, there are negative consequences to this approach.

In his book, *Glow Kids: How Screen Addiction Is Hijacking Our Kids—and How to Break the Trance*, Nicholas Kardaras writes about his experience as a therapist counseling children and teens. His stories are shocking and heartbreaking—kids who won't leave their rooms or their homes, kids who have become violent toward their parents, kids who have become obese, kids who can't sleep, kids who can barely have a conversation with another human being.

He cites research studies from brain scans that suggest tech exposure can "alter brain structure . . . in exactly the same way that drugs can," continuing, "people who had been diagnosed with Internet Addiction Disorder had myelin (white matter) integrity abnormalities in brain regions involving executive attention, decision making, and emotional generation."[2]

Kardaras argues that even the "average" kid can become hooked on screens.[3] "The kid without the lousy home life or internal demons can get trapped by addiction too. Regardless of why you do it, if you drink too much or play dopamine-activating video games all day, addiction can suck you in as well."[4] Kardaras notes that social isolation makes people more susceptible to alcohol and drug addiction. He believes this is also true for addiction to games.

"How many kids today feel adrift and purposeless?" Kardaras asks. Noting also the "hyperindividualist, hypercompetitive" society we live in, he says, if you "mix in a little stress, social disconnect and the seductively addicting escapism of glowing screens"—it's not surprising that the result is technology addiction.[5]

Peter Whybrow, a neuroscientist and psychiatrist who runs the Semel Institute for Neuroscience and Human Behavior, says that screens are like "digital heroin" for kids. When I ask him about whether this is literally true, he suggests that people have become too hung up on the medical definition of an addiction. Instead, we have to step back and look at the way "these devices tie into a section of the brain that is ancient and reward-driven."

Whybrow says that the "brain is based on very simple principles. If something works for you, you want to do it again. If you get negative feedback, then you pause." Forget about iPads for a moment and just think about television, he says. "Children love to watch changing colors. With a television set, the colors are constantly shifting. Kids love that. It's something that will addict any child if you put it in front of them."

But it is parents who get to decide how their kids will actually spend their time. "One of the things you have to realize," says Whybrow, "is that 80 percent of what we do every day is driven by habit. If you give a child at the age of eighteen months a wooden spoon and a few other bits out of your kitchen, they will play." That will become the habit. "Before you know it, they have a realm of fascinating stories about teddy and how teddy keeps on spilling his tea. That's the normal way in which human development begins."

Whybrow argues children wouldn't bother to learn how to walk if they just had a button that would bring them everything. "If you give these gadgets to kids when they are tiny, their attention span will shorten. By the time you put them in school, they will find it extraordinarily boring. They haven't been taught to concentrate."

How many kids are affected by something that medical professionals might recognize as technology addiction? Megan Moreno, a pediatrician at Seattle Children's Hospital who has helped to craft new guidelines for technology use for the AAP, says fewer than 1 percent of kids have a true addiction. That number is surprisingly large. It means that at any reasonably large middle school or high school there will be a few kids who can't lead a normal life because of their need for screen time. Moreno says there are another 5–7 percent whose use of technology is "problematic."

By contrast, the National Institutes of Health report that 2.7 percent of young people age twelve to twenty have an alcohol use disorder.[6] As parents, we certainly spend a lot more energy worrying about whether our older children are using alcohol in harmful ways than technology. At least with alcohol, we have the support of the law and most other parents when it comes to policing our children. The same is not true of technology.

Why don't we hear more about the fact that more than one in twenty kids exhibit a medically problematic use of technology? Why don't we hear more about the one in one hundred kids who could be diagnosed as having an actual addiction to technology?

Some experts believe that there is not a lot parents can do. Indeed, technology affects different kids in different ways. There is no magic number of hours or an Internet filter that will ensure your children will never fall into this category. (The same is also true of alcohol, of course.) There have been no studies showing that kids who play one kind of game will be fine and those who play another will be at risk. There is no single social media platform that ensures kids are safe and well adjusted.

The only thing that can really affect kids' relationship to technology is seriously curtailing it. Eliminating screen time during the week, limiting it to a couple of hours on the weekend, picking days to be technology free, putting off the purchase of a phone for a child, ending unsupervised use of technology, postponing or banning the use of social media, monitoring kids' communications on all platforms—these are, unfortunately, the only known ways to keep our kids out of harm's way. Many kids will be fine even without these restrictions, and some kids will fall into trouble even with them. But as parents, it's time for us to stop playing the odds.

Again and again in my interviews, experts tell me that there is no harm—not a single study—that finds kids who are *not* given screens experience problems as a result. Kids *without* screens don't exhibit more behavioral problems. They are *not* falling behind academically. They are *not* having trouble getting into college or finding employment. They are *not* losing focus in school or even becoming social outcasts.

Perhaps all this seems obvious, but it bears noting because in our attempts to weigh the costs and benefits of technology, we never seem to get around to suggesting that there are no discernible costs to withholding technology. In reality, there are abundant upsides to having our kids spend their time on other pursuits. So why don't the specialists on children and technology—the doctors and researchers, the psychologists and parenting experts—want to talk about the other side of this equation? The short answer seems to be that they don't want parents to feel guilty.

"I don't think parents should question their technology practices," says Heather Kirkorian of the Cognitive Development and Media Research Lab at the University of Wisconsin. "I think it's unrealistic and stresses parents more than it should to think the kids should never be exposed to screens." She worries that "some parents feel guilty if their kids" are exposed to the slightest bit of technology.

Similarly, the Tablet Project's Tim Smith says he worries when "I read some of the commentary on parent advice. They compare screen time and tablet use in children to some kind of parental abuse or neglect." He believes it is important to push back against this notion and instead suggest that parents give their kids technology "in moderation."

Rachel Barr says that she worries parents give "absolute prescriptions around media in a way that is not true with other caregiving practices." Barr worries that the "drug analogy" is not helpful for parents. "The world will not end" if your child spends some time on a device.

The concerns of these researchers are understandable. They see the culture of "parent shaming" around us. If you fail to give your kids organic food, if you put them in day care for too many hours, if you let them yell in a restaurant, or if you let them walk to school alone, there are people out there willing to call you out at every turn. They will yell at you in public or (perhaps worse) post videos of your bad parenting on social media.

Pediatricians and parenting experts don't want to add to the burdens of parents who are already stressed out and feeling like inferior mothers and fathers. But by holding back—by never simply saying that when it comes to screen time less is more—they are not giving parents the best information. They are taking away our agency to make the best decisions for our children. They are only adding to the chorus of voices in business, in education, and in our community who want us to throw our hands up and hand over the devices.

But who are these experts fooling? We know that screens are affecting our children in adverse ways, because we know they are affecting us, too. Many adults are trying to figure out how to cut back on their phone game addictions. In 2015, New York's public radio station, WNYC, launched the "Bored and Brilliant Project," in which host Manoush Zomorodi encourages listeners to be more mindful of the time they spend on their phones. As an experiment, she deleted an app called *Two Dots* from her phone after realizing how much time she was wasting on it and how little she was getting out of it. As one professor of cognitive psychology explained to her, "If you play *Ms. Pac-Man* a lot, you'll get better at *Mr. Pac-Man* and video games where you have to move through a maze. But you won't get better at *Space Invaders* or some real task like filling out your tax forms."[7]

The fact that these games are on mobile devices means that the temptation is always there. No respectable adult would spend hours in an arcade playing *Pac-Man* on a giant arcade machine, but on a phone? Well, no one can shame you if they think you're answering work emails. In 2014, a British member of Parliament, Nigel Mills, was caught playing *Candy Crush* for more than two and a half hours on his tablet during a House of Commons work and pensions committee meeting.[8]

.  .  .  .

We can see the effect that digital devices have on our kids, on our families, and on ourselves. And we can make a conscious choice to stop, or at least to slow down. Some of the parents I've interviewed had always planned to limit their kids' use of technology. But others have started to reverse habits that have been developed over years or even decades. It has not been easy, but many have faced obstacles far greater than I have. Their stories have inspired me to wonder about whether it's possible to make a different set of choices for my family, to find like-minded parents, and to create a culture where those choices are the norm as opposed to the exception.

In the survey I conducted in 2016, for 85 percent of parents whose oldest child was six, technology was either entertainment or a "distraction" while parents were doing something else. But their use of technology had evolved over time.

"Our oldest child had very minimal technology exposure," says Katy, the mother of a four-year-old and a one-year-old. "It's hard to preserve that for the youngest." Like many parents, she wonders, "How can we deal with the fact that we want to let our older one watch an educational program but we don't want our youngest one exposed yet?"

Liz, a mother of three in Indianapolis, recalls the same dynamic with her oldest. "I didn't have her until I was thirty-five," she says of her eleven-year-old daughter. "I was gung ho about being a parent. The pediatrician said no more than twenty minutes of television per day, so she didn't watch any. We did a lot of puzzles. We would go to the library, do story time. There's a wonderful children's museum. I was a control freak about technology. But as each child came along," she says, "I loosened my grip." This kind of intensive parenting is hard to sustain with more than one child.

There are piles of research showing that firstborn children have advantages that their younger siblings do not. Much of it stems from the fact that older children have their parents' undivided attention, even if it's for a short period of time. Parents also tend to be more intentional about their actions when it comes to older kids.

According to a 2013 paper from the National Bureau of Economic Research, "On average, mothers with two children were almost 8 percent less likely to say that their second child was one of the best in his class." The researchers, V. Joseph Hotz of Duke University and Juan Pantano of Washington University, found that "earlier-born children also had higher scores on the Peabody Individual Achievement Test and the Peabody Picture Vocabulary Test at age ten."[9]

The authors note that earlier-born siblings are more likely to be "subject to rules about TV watching and to face more intense parental monitoring regarding homework" and that "mothers are more likely to report that they would increase the supervision of one of their children in the event that child brought home a worse than expected report card when the child in question was one of her earlier-born children."[10]

The vast majority of parents I spoke to confirm this dynamic when it comes to technology. As Katie, a mother of three, told me, "My seven-year-old didn't watch much television at all until she was two. And then the only things she saw were *Sesame Street* and *Thomas the Tank Engine*." Her four-year-old and three-year-old, though, have had a much different experience. They watch Disney Junior, Sprout, and Nick Jr. They get to watch a show in the morning while the family is getting ready to leave the house. They watch while their mother is making dinner. And sometimes if Katie has to make a conference call for work after they come home from school, the three get to watch then as well. This is not a new phenomenon. My own parents report sticking me in front of the television for the first time just before the age of two, shortly after my younger sister was born.

None of this makes Katie (or my mother) poor parents. But when she talks about her younger children's experience, she does speak with a certain sense of regret about the different experience that her younger children are having. It is a joke among parents, especially those with more than two kids, that there are few pictures of the youngest ones, that they raise themselves. A neighbor of mine told me that she used to be very concerned about hygiene when her oldest child was a baby, sanitizing all the surfaces in the house and cleaning regularly. But with her third child, her only rule was "don't lick the driveway."

Even if they are not evident in school performance, there may be some benefits to the laissez-faire approach to parenting that younger siblings receive. Having parents who are not on top of them all the time may lead kids to experience greater independence at a younger age. They may be less anxious than their older siblings. There are certain advantages to being born into a family where parents are more confident and knowledgeable about parenthood. Not every tantrum will send the family into chaos. Not every sneeze will necessitate a trip to the pediatrician.

But should we be satisfied with a "don't lick the driveway" approach to these younger kids when it comes to technology? Increasing screen time seems to be the default way to deal with the demands of multiple children who want our attention at the same time. Linda, the mother of an eight-year-old girl and a five-year-old boy, recalls that she remembers relying on *Martha Speaks*, a PBS cartoon about a talking dog, to entertain her daughter while she nursed her son. "I could feed Charlie and not have her underfoot."

The word "underfoot" resonated with a lot of parents I spoke to. I remember trying to breastfeed my son while my two-year-old daughter wanted my attention. I complained to her ineffectively that I didn't have any hands free. That she needed to just wait. I would search for things that would occupy her for twenty minutes at a time, but two-year-olds are rarely occupied for such stretches without some adult feedback. Unless they are watching television.

So what can we do instead? First, it's useful to run a little thought experiment. Imagine what life was like for our grandparents or even our parents. As Marie Winn writes in *The Plug-In Drug*, "Before television, training children to play alone for periods of time was a vital part of parenthood. . . . This was not because parents thought this was particularly good for the child's development, but because they desperately needed those chunks of time for their own purposes."[11]

Winn suggests that parents watched their children carefully to see what would entertain them and then provided the necessary materials to accomplish this. Depending on the age, this might include blunt scissors, buttons, magazines, and so on. Before my daughter had learned to walk, she developed a love for ripping up newspapers—I can't say if this was a comment on my chosen profession or not—but a Sunday *New York Times* could keep her occupied for almost half an hour. She was filthy with newsprint at the end and the floor was a mess, but it was well worth it from my perspective. As Winn notes, a mother offers these activities "spurred not entirely by devotion to her child's happiness, but also by a certain amount of healthy self-interest."[12]

Winn also remarks on the disappearance of the nap as a reason parents feel pressured to provide their children with more screen time. For the first two years of childhood, most parents and caretakers revere the nap as a sacred time. They

*Tips for Cutting Back*

Embrace the mess. Screen time is always tempting because when kids are done with the iPad there's nothing to clean up. So give yourself a break. If the kids are entertaining themselves with blocks or dolls or art projects, don't worry about the cleanup until the end of the day.

will not make plans to leave the house or even have noise around the house during the hours of the nap. It can be difficult when children around the age of three stop needing the nap, as parents still need them to have one. Winn says, "This is why parents of the past persevered in their efforts to retain the nap in spite of the child's initial resistance. . . . Parents succeeded in gradually turning the sleep nap into a quiet-play nap, during which time children were to remain in their room, playing or listening to music or dreaming or puttering about quietly." Remarkably, Winn notes, parents were able to keep this up until children went off to elementary school.[13]

For many parents, though, television time has replaced quiet time. While they may see an hour on the couch as a kind of downtime for children—they are sitting still and being mostly quiet—the effects of replacing time alone dreaming or puttering around with screen time can be large.

In addition, Winn argues that watching television represents an entirely different state of consciousness for children than either being awake and playing or being asleep. She points to something I found from personal experience and in many of my interviews. When a screen is taken away or turned off, children become very cranky.

Even if they are not sleeping, something was lost when parents eliminated children's quiet time in their room and replaced it with television. Playing quietly alone can actually be an important part of children's development.

Early on in the 2015 hit movie *Joy*, we see the protagonist at the age of ten or so reach into a box of paper figures she created on her own—a tree, a bird, a fence—and start to tell her friend a story about them. The figures aren't fancy—the paper is all white—but they stand on their own. After listening, the friend suggests that all Joy needs now is a prince.

"No, I don't need a prince," she replies. "This is a special power." It's true that Joy, who is based on Joy Mangano (now a multimillionaire inventor of a variety of best-selling household products), does have a kind of special power. Nothing supernatural, though—just a great imagination and the tenacity to harness it.

But if the movie is accurate, she had access to some things that many kids today do not. She had time to herself to daydream and play and the ability to live in a world largely free of electronic distractions. Though her mother is constantly watching soap operas, Joy is more interested in using household items—paper, tape, crayons—to invent things. Her first invention was a glow-in-the-dark flea collar to make pets more visible to cars at night.

Though Joy came from a working-class household, it turns out that her childhood shares some elements with many of the world's creative geniuses. In their book *Imagination and Play in the Electronic Age*, Yale researchers Dorothy Singer and Jerome Singer note, "Autobiographical reports or direct interviews conducted with eminent writers, inventors and scientists demonstrate that their early experiences with play in childhood ... are important features of their creative process."[14]

They describe how we all have fleeting thoughts or day-dreams, but the people later regarded as geniuses are able to pay close attention to those fantasies and harness them for innovation. The authors cite the example of Nikola Tesla, inventor of alternating current motors and generators, who wrote, "When I get an idea I start at once building it up in my imagination. I change the construction, make improvements and operate the device in my mind."[15]

Getting a young child to engage in pretend play can be frustrating at first. It can take them a while to work up to being able to do it for any sustained period of time. But developing these habits early can be the key to certain kinds of success later on. "Our own research on daydreaming and imaginal processes," Singer and Singer write, "has shown that individuals who show a constructive, positive use of their imagination are those who score higher on questionnaire measures of openness. . . . Perhaps our adult imaginative capacities and our ability to control them may take their primordial origin in children's make-believe play." Finally, they note, "there are indications that children who, early on, engage in pretend play are also likely to be more amiable, persistent, and conscientious."[16]

Of course there is nothing about babies and toddlers watching an hour or two of television a day that precludes them from engaging in pretend play. When being home with a young child, it can seem as though the hours go by so slowly, but when all is said and done, there are relatively few that are not spent eating, sleeping, bathing, doing chores, running errands, and so forth. Once children begin preschool a few hours a day, the chunks of time shrink significantly.

Indeed, modern parents go to great lengths to make sure that we don't have unstructured time with our kids and that they don't have unstructured time alone. And children build their expectations accordingly. When I am home on a weekend day with my kids, they want to know what the plan will be. When their father is in charge, they are more likely to hang around the house, playing with toys or running around outside. Sometimes I have to remind myself these are the same kids. But just as kids expect to behave differently at school and at home, different adults have a different effect. If a college girl comes over to babysit, the kids expect her to play board games, teach them how to make paper fortune-tellers, and give them her undivided attention for hours on end.

Geula Zamist, the early childhood director, says she used to think that parents were signing up for so many mommy and me classes because they wanted to meet other moms. And certainly it's true that we don't meet other parents in our neighborhoods as we once did. But over time, she started to realize that parents "had no idea how to play with their kids." Or even "that they were afraid to be left alone to play with their kids."

Indeed, it has become obvious to her that even during mommy and me classes, plenty of mothers are not playing with their children at all. Some are talking to other mothers—reasonably enough—but many more are just checking their phones. These days she talks to parents at the beginning of the year about their expectations for the class—and hers. She asks them to see it as a "sacred time" to play with their children. By which she also means, "put your phones away, please."

The idea that parents have forgotten how to play with their kids first struck her about a decade ago when she went to buy a set of multicolored, multisized rings for her baby granddaughter. She was surprised when she opened them to find a set of instructions in the box, which read, in part: "Show your child the red one. Hold it up. Say, 'This is the red one.'"

While there are probably some parents who have become

so reliant on technology that they don't know how to engage a child with a simple toy, I think it's more likely that parents have simply become used to the notion that electronic entertainment is easier. Even if children will ultimately entertain themselves by ripping up paper or knocking down blocks, there is a certain investment of time that is required early on in the process. It's not just that you have to observe what a child likes and find the material. Often, you have to show them how to play with it. Even with something as simple as plastic rings. Oh, and you have to clean it up. This is not true of the growing number of electronic toys out there. Even the ones that are connected to the Internet.

When the AAP recommended no screen time at all for children under two years old in 2011, many parents told me that their pediatricians had passed on this advice to them and they had taken it quite seriously. While some of those parents were already inclined to limit screen time, others said that it pushed them to set firm rules. New parents, not surprisingly, put a lot of stock in the things their pediatricians say to them. All the more reason why the AAP should have gone further, recommending no screen time for kids who are even older than age two. Many parents might have allowed some, but at least they would be aware of the standard.

The truth is that many parents aren't getting the message. A mother in a wealthy suburb of New York posted this on a Facebook group: "Good Morning Moms. Time has come that we need to purchase a tablet for our toddler, [who] will be 3 in July. Curious to what everyone has gotten there [sic] toddlers; a plain tablet where u add apps or a Nabi or other kid friendly tablet. Thank you in advance." The dozens of responses were divided among Kindles, iPads and Nabis, but no one suggested that two was a little young for a tablet.

Ashley, a nanny living in Pittsburgh with a baby of her own

now, says that she attended story time at the local library with her fifteen-month-old son only to find out that the libraries were handing iPads to the toddlers. "He was completely distracted from singing the songs. He loved it. He couldn't look away."

The presence of tablets and smartphones has made it much more difficult to restrict screen time because screens are always available—even at the library. Perhaps even more so than when we are at home, being out with a child means that we need to get things done. We are running errands or trying to speak with other adults. At home we can provide them with toys or put them in cribs or behind gates. But at the supermarket or the dry cleaner or when speaking to older siblings' teachers or, ahem, traffic cops, it would be easier if our children were occupied. And so suddenly what started out as an hour of television in the morning while a parent cleaned up the kitchen after breakfast or took a shower turns into three hours over the course of a day, whenever a distraction is needed.

Most parents I interviewed say this is not what they intended. Life gets faster and faster and in order to keep up, they need to find more and more ways to keep the kids busy. The problem starts younger and younger. These parents are looking for a way to stop what they see as the inevitable slide toward more and more time on screens. But how?

Kara, a mother of four in Washington, DC, recalls when her oldest daughter was two years old. She hadn't watched much television when she was young, but then Kara's husband was in Iraq for an extended period of time. "I was working. And when I came home I needed her to be quiet for thirty minutes. That's when television entered into our lives." She and her husband took in a foster child shortly after that. "During that year," Kara recalls, "I used screen time as a crutch. When parenting became too difficult, I couldn't cope."

But what started out as a solution to a crisis—being a single working parent with a spouse halfway across the world in a war zone—became a regular routine. Even after her husband returned, her kids (now ages eight, five, three, and one) were "always asking to watch something." Kara recalls, "It was the priority of the day. When are we going to watch? Who is going to pick?"

A couple of years later, after their foster child left, Kara says, "it was a particularly traumatic time for us." She said that she and her husband decided to "reassess the family's culture." That's when she came to an important realization: "I was choosing not to parent in difficult moments by giving them something to watch."

What does it mean when we choose not to parent? It may be that we are not engaging with kids, not disciplining them, not encouraging them, not even observing what they're doing. It may be that we have given up authority and we are trying to be their friends instead. It may be that we are distracting ourselves from the needs of our children. Instead of thinking about what will help them in the long run, we are thinking of what will keep them quiet in the short run. Technology allows us to do all of those things more easily.

So Kara and her husband stepped back. And what they decided was that screens would only be available to their children on the weekends, and even then they would mostly be reserved for family movie nights. They keep their one television in the house behind the couch and generally take it out only when Kara's husband wants to watch a big sporting event. For about two years they have largely kept to this rule. "We talk about family culture," says Kara. "People are more important than devices."

Kara has some friends who have adopted a similar mindset when it comes to technology, but there are plenty of people in her community who ask her how she and her husband enforce these rules. "Everyone has their own hardships. I remember wondering that too when technology was my coping mechanism."

But now Kara has decided to cope without giving her kids technology and even using it too much herself. She's giving up her smartphone and going back to a basic cell phone. "The way I use a smartphone, it's totally an addiction," she tells me. "I know a lot of people on playgrounds are working," checking in with bosses, while they are trying to supervise children. But Kara says, "That's not me. I have the luxury of being a stay-at-home mom."

Kara's husband has a demanding job that requires him to stay in constant contact with his work, and he is on his smartphone a lot. But they have explained that to their kids too. "There is a difference between adults and kids."

There is nothing special about Kara. Her family is middle class, and they send their kids to a neighborhood Lutheran school. Her peer group is generally more permissive when it comes to technology. But she has seen what so many of us have become blind to—that technology fundamentally alters our relationship with our children. That, almost without noticing, we have become addicted to our screens. They have become an integral part of our social life and our work life. But they have also enabled us "not to parent." It is time to rethink our approach to technology, if for no other reason than that.

When I started working on this project, I called a friend of mine, Noah. He has two teenage stepchildren from his husband's previous marriage, and he has been helping to raise them for the better part of a decade. They are great kids—smart and happy and ambitious. But a few years ago, their parents noticed that, as Noah says, "the kids would get sucked into the screen. The amount of time they were on their phones was ridiculous. We had to be more proactive about time management. There had to be an awareness of how long they were on it."

Dialing it all back has been a long road and not without bumps. So it was interesting that when the two had a daughter together three years ago they took "a different approach." As Noah describes, "Talia's three. She's never watched TV. She'll see a three-minute video of a song in a different language every couple of weeks. She can't get enough of reading books, even though she can't really read. The school we send her to is exploratory learning. There are chickens and rabbits and no technology in the classroom." Not every parent gets to bring up a new baby knowing what teenagers will be like. But Talia is clearly reaping the benefits of a family that has seen where too much technology can lead and decided to go a different route.

## CHAPTER 8

# Less Technology, More Independence

■ ■ ■ ■

W HAT WOULD IT MEAN for kids—and their parents—to disconnect? Not just for a significant part of their day but for longer—much longer?

"I want to be careful not to demonize electronics," Richard Louv tells me. Louv, who is the author of the best-selling book *Last Child in the Woods*, says that there are two problems with blaming the problems of kids today on the overuse of technology. First, he says, anything parents want to ban, kids want to do more. But more seriously, he argues, the over-reliance on technology is not the cause. It's merely one of the effects of the problems in our parenting and the problems in our culture.

Parents who want their children to have a head start on learning may have lost perspective on how kids at their age develop healthily and what the best ways are to encourage that. As Louv and others have pointed out, it is fear that is driving many of our parenting decisions—fear not just that our children won't get ahead but also fear for their safety. For a mother in inner-city Chicago, this makes a lot of sense. But, thankfully, few Americans live in neighborhoods where drive-by shootings and gang violence are a regular feature of life. In fact, most Americans are safer than they have been in decades.

Lenore Skenazy, the author of *Free-Range Kids, Giving Our Children the Freedom We Had Without Going Nuts with Worry*, continues to amass statistics on her website about how safe our kids are. Per FBI Uniform Crime Reports, all violent crime dropped 48 percent between 1993 and 2012. During the same period, homicides were down over 50 percent and forcible rape down over 34 percent. Among children ages two to seventeen, physical assault was down 33 percent between 2003 and 2011, according to the University of New Hampshire Crimes Against Children Research Center. And rape, attempted or completed, was down 43 percent during that time. As for child abductions, the statistics are infinitesimal. Of the 800,000 children reported "missing" in the United States each year, 115 are the result of a stranger snatching a child.[1]

So why are kids not allowed to play outside by themselves? Why won't we let them wander through the woods? Why does every outside adventure involve several layers of sunscreen and bug spray and an adult walking within five feet of children at all times? There is a confluence of factors at work here—not least of which is our overly litigious society, in which no school, law enforcement agency, or other government bureaucracy wants to be held accountable if anything does happen to a child.

But Louv adds other theories. He suggests that nature itself is now so unexplored that many adults and children have a deep-seated fear of it. We moved from a rural society to a suburban and urban one in the second half of the twentieth century, so kids are less likely to encounter the natural world in their day-to-day lives. He says that popular culture has also had some effect here, with movies like *The Blair Witch Project* suggesting that nature is something to be afraid of.

He even suggests that ironically, environmentalists themselves have contributed to the problem. Since whenever we speak to children about nature, it is usually about some apocalyptic event that is going to befall the planet, and children get the message that nature is basically one big impending disaster.

But what about the idea of enjoying nature? Of wandering through the forests in their own backyards? Kids can no longer build tree houses because they're too dangerous and might damage a tree. They can't go fishing or hunting because they might kill something. They can't wander aimlessly around outside because it won't build their college résumé.

When we spend too much time fearing or pitying nature and not enough time enjoying it, something is lost. Study after study suggests that spending time outside reduces stress for children and adults. Even having a view of nature from a hospital room has been shown to reduce recovery time. A much-cited study, published in 1984 in *Science* by environmental psychologist Roger Ulrich, looked at the records of patients recovering from gallbladder surgery. All other things being equal, those with bedside windows looking out on trees healed, on average, a day faster; needed less pain medication; and had fewer complications than patients who looked at a brick wall.[2]

In an interview with *Scientific American* about the utility of gardens in hospital settings, Clare Cooper Marcus, an emeritus professor of architecture at University of California Berkeley said, "Spending time interacting with nature in a well-designed garden won't cure your cancer or heal a badly burned leg. But there is good evidence it can reduce your levels of pain and stress—and, by doing that, boost your immune system in ways that allow your own body and other treatments to help you heal."[3]

Other research has found that spending time in nature increases one's attention span. And in an era when millions of children are being prescribed drugs for ADHD, it is worth noting that there might be ways to help them with fewer side effects.

Indeed, Louv is fond of saying that when he was a kid "nature was my Ritalin." But that prescription is increasingly uncommon. A survey by professors at Manhattanville College on eight hundred mothers revealed that almost three-quarters of them recall playing outside every day when they were children. But only a quarter of them say their kids play outside every day.[4]

Cameron, the mother of an eight-year-old boy, is probably among those. She recalls that her mother was very strict about her outdoor play and her use of technology. Over the summer, "I can't remember her letting us watch a single half hour of television. It was a very '80s childhood. She would say, 'Don't come back into the house unless you have to pee. And really, you can pee at someone else's house.'" Her son plays outside at school, but at home his nearest neighbors are across a busy street, they're not his age, and they're probably not outside anyway. "I could throw him in the backyard," she says, "but he'd be alone."

The time that kids do spend outside more often is in an organized sport rather than in nature. Don Sabo, a professor at D'Youville College in Buffalo, found that 75 percent of boys and 69 percent of girls from eight to seventeen took part in organized sports in 2008—playing on at least one team or in one club.[5] And that doesn't even count youth soccer and T-ball teams that regularly include four- and five-year-olds on their rosters. It's one of the little remarked upon ironies of our age that childhood obesity has skyrocketed at the same time as kids' participation in organized sports has reached its zenith. If you spend a few hours at Little League games, you'll notice a lot of the time is spent standing around.

An older gentleman I interviewed recently told me that he is a big financial supporter of the Boy Scouts in part because you can do well at it and enjoy being outside even if you're not an athletic kid. "What it takes to earn a badge is hard work." Sadly, Boy Scout membership has been in decline. The Girl Scouts, meanwhile, have focused less and less on outdoor skills. They seem to be more concerned with earning badges in teaching tolerance or financial literacy than pitching a tent or identifying birds.

Now the kids who are not adept at sports have few alternatives. So they just sit inside and play video games. In his 2016 book *The Collapse of Parenting*, psychiatrist Leonard Sax tells the story of a young man who tried out for his high school football team but couldn't run a mile in under twelve minutes. While the coach said he would work with the kids who were out of shape, the boy decided he'd rather play football video games at home, and his father simply went along with his plan. Surely it's time for parents to start taking responsibility here.

Louv tells me that the point is not to eliminate technology but to provide children with some balance. He has written extensively about "attention restoration." Our brains, he says, "get burned out" from too much time on a screen. While he recognizes that we have to use computers for our work and daily life, "the best way to counteract" that burnout, "is to pay a different kind of attention. It's a shortcut to restoring your brain."

Louv's advice is based on something called attention restoration theory. Developed in the 1980s by professors Stephen and Rachel Kaplan of the University of Michigan, attention restoration theory (ART) posits that we have two different kinds of attention. Directed attention is what we use to accomplish tasks like studying or writing—and too much of that results in what's called "directed attention fatigue."

As Stephen Kaplan writes in a paper called "The Restorative Benefits of Nature: Toward an Integrative Framework": Any time one has worked intensely on a project and subsequently finds oneself mentally exhausted, one has experienced this unwelcome state. The typical state of mind of students at the end of a semester is a familiar example. In fact, even a thoroughly enjoyable project, if sufficiently intense and sufficiently prolonged, is likely to lead to this same outcome.[6]

Kaplan and others have suggested that from an evolutionary perspective, there is a reason that we only have so much ability to pay this kind of attention. "To be able to pay attention by choice to one particular thing for a long period of time would make one vulnerable to surprises. Being vigilant, being alert to one's surroundings may have been far more important than the capacity for long and intense concentration."

There are different ways that children—and adults—can recover from the kind of fatigue this creates. Sleep is obviously one of them. But the researchers who developed ART suggest that time outside in nature is a good way to accomplish this. Kids should pay *a different kind of* attention.

The idea of nature having a restorative effect on our minds goes back a long way. In the *Principles of Psychology*, written well over one hundred years ago, William James speaks of "voluntary" and "involuntary" attention. The former, he writes, occurs in school settings, when students are engaged in dull subjects. "Voluntary attention, in short, is only a momentary affair. The process, whatever it is, exhausts itself in the single act." But involuntary attention—or passive attention as it has become more commonly known—involves a kind of fascination with the world at large.

James notes that "sensitiveness to immediately exciting sensorial stimuli characterizes the attention of childhood and youth." Indeed, these years in preschool and early elementary school are a time when parents and teachers devote great effort to reducing this sensitivity. We are trying to redirect children's attention away from the strange, pretty, and bright things toward more academic pursuits, pursuits that require their voluntary attention.

But maybe they're not ready. Louv argues that we are actually limiting the development of our senses by "creating environments in schools and home in which we spend more and more of life in front of screens." To him, it seems as if we are "unconsciously trying to push out and push away senses we don't know we have in order to focus just on eyes and ears." But our other senses, Louv suggests, "are atrophying." For example, he says, we are losing "spatial sense," the ability to determine where we are, to imagine the scale of the area around us.

He goes so far as to say that "if we're continuing to create [stripped-down] environments, spending that much energy pushing away those senses," that is the "definition of being less alive." And he wonders, "What parent wants their child to be less alive?"

By engaging more of our senses, Louv believes, nature has the ability to make it seem as though time is slowing down. You can see this represented in movies sometimes. When danger is approaching, "the leaf in front of a cowboy's eyes would be very clear. He would notice wind. These are the details you don't usually think about." When we are in nature and paying a more involuntary kind of attention to our surroundings, there is more information coming into our senses.

When we are older, we are always saying that time seems to fly by. When we are young, though, time seems slower because we are absorbing more information through passive attention to our surroundings. Our sense of awareness is heightened when we are younger. Technology seems to have the opposite effect, speeding up time through distraction.

I noticed the effect of technology on time a few years ago. When our evenings were divided up into half-hour increments, there seemed to be a frantic sense about them—how many shows could we squeeze in? Who would get to pick? How many minutes before bedtime would we have to turn it off? After we eliminated screen time during the week, things seemed to slow down. When homework was done and the kids were reading or playing games with each other and us, things seemed calmer.

There is a countercultural movement developing around the idea that kids need to spend more time outside, exploring nature, independently, without constant supervision. In addition to the free-range parent movement and Louv's Children and Nature Network, there are also books like *How to Raise a Wild Child* by Scott Sampson, which is more of a manual for ways to get kids to engage with nature.

There are thousands of nature-based preschools across the country now as well. The models include Montessori, Waldorf, and Reggio Emilia. The last has grown in popularity, particularly in upper-class enclaves in recent years. Interestingly, it began in postwar Italy, in a town that had largely been destroyed by fascist rulers and then by wartime bombings. The citizens of the town built a school from the rubble of what remained.

Writing about the history of the Reggio model in a 2013 article in the *Atlantic*, Emily Chertoff explains:

> Born out of a desire to provide children with an enriching environment, the Reggio schools came to emphasize art and the beauty of the classroom. Children were encouraged to pursue their own

projects and to use materials from nature in their work. Maybe because the parents developed their first teaching methods ad hoc, Reggio Emilia never developed a specific curriculum. More than anything, the schools were designed to bring color and activity into the lives of children of war.[7]

It seems strange to think that American children in the twenty-first century need the same kinds of educational enrichment that children in postwar Europe did. But divorced as they are from the beauty of the natural world, this model seems to have something important to offer. The preschool my children attended adopted the Reggio model a couple of years ago. And while there are some things that seemed a little odd—the bulletin boards favored natural materials over more vibrant colored construction paper and the kids were expected to play outside even when it was raining—the model seemed—as a whole—to inspire lots of interesting questions from the kids. It seemed very much like what preschool offered in the 1970s when I attended—a lot of time for play.

· · · ·

In our haste to give kids an academic advantage, we have cut off an important vehicle for learning. Not only can time outside in nature and away from screens provide them with a way to develop their senses, it can also provide them with an important respite from the long periods of directed attention we require of them.

To find out how nature can be integrated into education, I took a trip to Prescott, Arizona. In the far corner of the desolate-looking yard outside Mountain Oak Charter School, a boy of nine or ten is digging a hole. A few other children are standing nearby, periodically checking his progress and taking a turn with the shovel.

Mountain Oak is a prekindergarten through eighth grade charter school that offers an education inspired by Waldorf, a progressive model that encourages exploration of the natural world and rejects the use of technology in the classroom and even in the home. When I ask later in the afternoon about the ditch digging, eighth-grade teacher Jeffrey Holmes smiles. "Oh, they're playing *Minecraft*," he says, referring to the popular online game. Last year "they had a whole system of ditches and they were bartering with rocks too."

Waldorf private schools have been around for almost a hundred years—the first was launched by educator Rudolf Steiner in Germany. But they have been experiencing a resurgence in the United States, where Waldorf has become popular with wealthy parents, including Silicon Valley types, who are attracted by the more simplified approach to learning.

It is not simply the academic approach of Waldorf that makes it different. If you spend any time at one of these schools, you will see how this low-tech teaching method also seems to affect the way students relate to one another. Some of the kids play basketball during recess the way they would at any other school, but pretend play for both boys and girls seems to extend to later ages. The older kids are not looking at phones during their school breaks or playing video games. They are building things or examining plants or creating obstacle courses for others to try.

All of this is encouraged by their activities in class, which often involve recitations of poems or other public speaking. Each year each class also puts on a play where everyone is required to participate. The kids I interview seem unusually personable and completely capable of interacting with adults. They do not seem to have much use for communicating with their classmates outside of school. A few of them have cell phones or use the ones that belong to their parents, but it is mostly to arrange times and places to meet up.

## Tips for Cutting Back

Deprivation is not sustainable, substitution is. If you're going to take away technology, you have to give your kids other things—more time outside, more time with you, more low-tech toys.

Ethan Windecker, an eighth grader at Mountain Oak, says that he has a phone that he occasionally uses to send funny videos to his friend. At his old school, which he left in sixth grade, he says, "there was a lot of texting and always something going on. . . . Your phone is always on [inside class and out]. It's kind of irritating after a while." His classmate, Brody Tubbs, meanwhile, says he has a phone that is not fully activated. While his friends occasionally text about sports and he likes to catch up with them, he says, "I don't have much use for social media or texting."

Talking to the kids at Mountain Oak, you can hear a certain kind of independence in their attitudes. Like any adolescents, they presumably care what their friends think, but not as urgently. There is nothing buzzing in their pocket alerting them to gossip or the latest trend or a party that everyone is going to. Communication is something that happens more often in person. It happens when they decide to initiate it.

A 2011 article in the *New York Times* describes the Peninsula Waldorf School, where "the chief technology officer of eBay sends his children. . . . So do employees of Silicon Valley giants like Google, Apple, Yahoo and Hewlett-Packard."[8] What do these tech gurus know that many American parents don't? For one thing, they believe that kids learn better with pens and paper and more human interaction. But they also see technology as a distraction, and they don't think that early exposure to it will make kids more competent with it.

One Google executive explained that he believes using technology is "super easy. It's like learning to use toothpaste. . . . At Google and all these places, we make technology as brain-dead easy to use as possible. There's no reason why kids can't figure it out when they get older."[9]

Over and over when I interviewed people who were engineers or software designers, the reaction was the same. Technology is great—and getting better all the time—but it's not something that they had at a young age and not something they think their kids need now in order to succeed. They want their kids to have the space to develop their minds and their social skills before entering the frantic world of communication and information that we adults must live with.

One of the most frequently passed around articles in the mommy blogosphere reveals that Steve Jobs didn't let his kids use the iPad. Writing in the *New York Times*, reporter Nick Bilton recalled asking Jobs when the device first came out: "So, your kids must love the iPad?"[10]

"'They haven't used it,' he told me. 'We limit how much technology our kids use at home.'" Jobs's reply left the reporter in "dumbfounded silence." Bilton, who went on to interview other tech gurus, received similar answers.

In a 2017 interview, Bill Gates said that he didn't allow his children to have cell phones until they were fourteen years old. They didn't allow phones at dinner and screen time was cut off well before bedtime. "You're always looking at how [smartphones] can be used in a great way—homework and staying in touch with friends—and also where it has gotten to excess," Gates explained.[11]

It's not merely people in Silicon Valley who have "seen the dangers of technology firsthand," as a former editor of *Wired* magazine put it.[12] It's every middle- and upper-class parent walking around with an iPhone. We are all well aware of the effects of too much screen time on our own ability to concentrate and our social interactions. And, even if we give in more often than we'd like, we don't want those effects for our kids.

In addition to eschewing technology, Waldorf schools tend to delay formal reading instruction—until around the age of seven—and testing and to reserve kindergarten entirely for imaginative play, especially with blocks and natural materials such as leaves and other things found outdoors. Students at all levels receive extensive instruction in music and art. They also do physical exercises in the classroom to break up their lessons. They work with their hands as well, learning woodworking and sewing, understanding how to use old-fashioned tools.

But this model is no longer limited to private education. In recent years, Waldorf-inspired charter schools have begun popping up—there are almost fifty—especially in the West. Mountain Oak is one of the older ones, launched in 1999. It serves about 150 students, about half of whom receive a free or reduced-price lunch.

Mountain Oak students perform at the state average on tests, but the school has been given an A grade by Arizona's state education department because of the academic improvement its students experience compared with their peers with similar backgrounds at public schools. Unlike parents at the private Waldorf schools, though, many Mountain Oak parents must be persuaded by teachers that the elimination of tablets, smartphones, and even television at home is an important part of this success.

Teachers at Mountain Oak say they can walk into a classroom and immediately tell who has been using devices at home. "We see it in their behavioral problems, their ability to reason, their cognitive skills, even their ability to communicate with other people," one teacher tells me. Jennifer McMillan, who teaches kindergarten, says she has to "have the conversation in a gentle way." Many of these parents simply don't understand the effects that staring at a screen can have on children's behavior and their ability to learn.

The teachers at Mountain Oak say they have the toughest time trying to reduce electronics and media use among children in single-parent households. Typically, these mothers tend to be younger and less educated, and it is very tempting after a long day at work to come home and turn on a screen to keep a child occupied. The teachers keep prodding anyway.

While there's evidence to suggest that poor children are slightly less likely to have access to laptops and tablets, those without are a pretty small slice of the population. In researching her book *Alone Together*, MIT professor Sherry Turkle says she was surprised by how widespread the use of devices was across class lines. She writes:

> Necessarily, my claims about new connectivity devices and the self apply to those who can afford such things. This turned out to be a larger group than I had originally supposed. For example, in a public high school study in the spring of 2008, every student across a wide range of economic and cultural situations had a mobile phone that could support texting. Most students had phones that could put them on the web.[13]

According to a 2015 Pew report, "Fully 87% of American teens ages 13 to 17 have or have access to a desktop or laptop computer." For families earning less than fifty thousand dollars a year, that number is 80 percent. As for a racial divide, Pew finds that African-American teenagers are more likely to own a smartphone than any other group of teens in America.[14]

What no one tells low-income families is this: the real digital divide is between parents who realize the harmful effects of technology on their children and try to limit them and those who don't. It's the difference between parents buying wooden blocks at Christmas and those racking up more credit card debt to buy a Leap Pad. Go into any upscale toy store, and you'll find it littered with pretend food, art supplies, and some simple costumes.

* * * *

These are real divides in our country. And when we talk about the inequalities in the United States today, these are the ones we should be thinking about. Many middle-class mothers and fathers understand that while technology may provide many benefits to children, they are nothing compared to the intellectual and social benefits of nonelectronic toys, of reading books, of time spent outside, and of communication with peers without the interference of technology. Not only are the parents at Mountain Oak and in other low-tech educational communities offering the next generation a better education without the distractions of technology, they are also helping them learn how to filter out some of the cultural noise that surrounds kids. And that, more than anything else, might be the real advantage a child can have today.

At the end of his work *The Disappearance of Childhood*, Neil Postman asks whether the individual "is powerless to resist what is happening" in the broader culture, whether, that is, there is any way to preserve childhood. To which he responds that there are parents "who are in effect defying the directives of their culture. Such parents are not only helping their children to have a childhood but are, at the same time, creating a sort of intellectual elite." He predicts that children who grow up in these homes "will, as adults, be much favored by business, the professions and the media themselves."[15]

In other words, without getting too conspiratorial about it, Postman argues that elites will ensure that their children remain elite through their restriction of media consumption. The adults in the higher echelons of society will limit their kids' access to the culture that they themselves have helped to perpetuate.

This means not simply that kids have less screen time watching television or playing on tablets. It also means that their communications with peers will be limited in some sense. In part that's because peers are the vehicle through which they can access the culture.

∎ ∎ ∎ ∎

In 2013, the *New York Times* profiled Melissa and Doug Bernstein, the founders of the toy company Melissa & Doug, which is now almost thirty years old. While the rest of the toy economy was tanking, Melissa & Doug was pulling in $325 million annually. "In a time when major corporations dominate the industry, making toys with all manner of batteries, digital gimmicks or movie tie-ins, the Bernsteins keep making money in wooden puzzles, coloring pads, blocks, trains and simple costumes (the police officer, the princess, the pirate). They hatch many of their ideas by watching children at play—often among their own brood of six."[16]

Today, Melissa & Doug toys are more ubiquitous, but a decade ago when I started attending baby showers and toddler birthday parties, the brand seemed to be part of some kind of secret code that wealthy Westchester mothers used to communicate with each other—like organic food. Their toys would last longer, be less annoying to listen to, and probably teach children more. Some of the parents worried about their kids' exposure to the chemicals in plastic, but most seemed happy to have something sturdy that kids would want to play with over and over.

So why do some parents give their kids electronic toys anyway? Melissa Bernstein told the *Times*, "Parents are so scared of having their kids say, 'I'm bored.' It's synonymous with, 'I'm a bad parent,' and so they never allow kids to feel boredom, which equals frustration, and so kids don't get to the point where they have to dig deeper and figure out what to do."[17] Melissa & Doug toys make kids dig deeper.

## Tips for Cutting Back

Spoil your children—just not with technology. Take them to a bookstore and let them pick out whatever they want. Take them to an art supply store or a sporting goods store and let them find some new paints or a bouncy ball. Make them feel indulged and they will be less resentful about the absence of screens.

If you look at other toy companies, you'll notice that the items on the market intended to teach science or math are not minicomputers but microscopes and abacuses. "Toys that help kids become global leaders," a list compiled by the website *Quartz* in 2014, includes building kits with wooden pieces or board games that are focused on strategy.[18] The only toys on this list that involve electronics are ones that allow kids to build their own robots.

"I'm really partial to hand tools and manipulating the world directly," Lowell Monke tells me. Monke, a professor of education at Wittenberg University, grew up on farm and learned how to build and fix things from a young age. "I have grandchildren," he laments "who unfortunately don't know how to swing a hammer." Just giving kids computers "does young people such a disservice. They're always thinking they have to have something to help them. They have to have complex tools, but that they can't understand how they work." Monke says our lack of hands-on knowledge "makes us slaves to the technology gurus." The end result, says Monke, is that our kids feel "helpless."

But not the kids at Waldorf schools, who seem to know how to work with tools, how to build and sew, how to read and draw, and how to speak to other people—even adults—without emoji's.

Felicia Fishback, who is recently divorced, has never liked video games, but once she started sending her four children to Mountain Oak, she realized that these were making her oldest son's behavior worse and hindering his academic performance. He had been diagnosed with ADHD and was gaining weight from a lack of physical activity. Now her children are not allowed any screen time during the week and a little on weekends. "Mountain Oak," she says, "has made me a better parent."

Sunshine Reilly, who lives on a farm near Mountain Oak and has a son in sixth grade there, recalls putting him in front of the television for hours a day when he was a toddler while she did chores. It wasn't until he started kindergarten that she understood that the screen time was hurting his ability to entertain himself, to enjoy books, and even to like playing outside.

. . . .

A couple of months after my son started second grade, I remember him pouring over an atlas on our family room floor. He asked me about finding Massachusetts on a map—that's where his grandparents live. When I told him to look further north, he seemed puzzled. "Simon, which direction is north?" I asked. Without hesitation, he answered, "Up." It was a perfectly logical answer for someone who liked maps but was used to seeing them pinned to the front of a classroom rather than actually using them to get places.

A few weeks after this conversation, I found myself at a state park in the suburbs of Philadelphia with a group of about thirty kids ranging from toddlers to teenagers. A young man in his twenties took out a map of the park and handed a few other copies to the kids. Then he took out his compass—a couple of the kids pulled out their own as well—and asked them which way we should go to get to the trail. The kids laid their maps on the ground and quickly found the answer. "That way is north," yelled one boy who looked to be about ten. "We need to head to the left up ahead."

Like many of the kids at the park that day, this boy seemed confident, knowledgeable about his surroundings, and happy to talk to other kids of different ages, not to mention their parents. He was curious and excited but also surefooted and eager to warn others about pitfalls on the trail ahead.

As parents, we often have moments where we think to ourselves, "I never want my kid to act like that." But occasionally we have moments where we look at other children and think, "I hope my child can do that too." I hope my child can be that generous and compassionate. I hope my child can look adults in the eye and speak clearly. I hope my child can work hard at something he or she finds frustrating. I hope that when my child leaves my home to make his way in the world that he or she can exercise good judgment and restraint but also love and enthusiasm and curiosity. I hope my child can be comfortable being alone but also enjoy the company of others, even if they are not exactly like him or her. I hope my child is willing to venture into unfamiliar territory and has some thoughts on navigating it.

Not every parent's hopes will be the same, but for the parents I've interviewed in the past few years, these are some of the aspirations that top the list. As goals, they are both eminently reasonable and amazingly difficult. But when you meet young adults in the world—interns, babysitters, swimming teachers, neighbors—it becomes clear quickly which of them are, to borrow a phrase, "ready to launch."

The kids gathered at the park that day are becoming the kind of independent, self-assured, happy, curious, sociable kids that many parents today say they want. Who were they? Mostly students from the Charlotte Mason Academy (CMA). Their parents homeschool them, but once or twice a week they gather to learn subjects their parents might not have the knowledge or resources to teach them. They were black and white and Asian. They were religious and secular. They were working class and upper-middle class.

When I arrived at the park, it was just after lunch and families were starting to gather at a group of picnic tables in the shade. Some children were sitting with sketchbooks open, drawing intricate pictures of flowers and leaves. Others were climbing trees. I know it sounds like a cliché of our helicopter age that parents don't let their kids climb trees anymore. But they really don't. And these kids were twenty feet up. With the exception of an occasional glance, no one was monitoring their progress. Meanwhile, back on the ground, I noticed some of the kids had taken off their shoes and were playing in the dirt. And a few had wandered down to a brook nearby—again, with no immediate supervision.

Launched in 2010, CMA meets on Fridays for "Nature Club." It has hired a couple of young men to lead the kids on hikes and teach them about some of the plants and animals they can see, as well as the ways rivers flow, rocks are formed, and so forth. The group was named after Charlotte Mason, a British educator at the turn of the twentieth century. Mason wrote several volumes on how and what to teach young people, and there are schools across the country and around the world that use her methodology. She did not like textbooks, believing that they were often written in tones too condescending to children. She thought oral presentations were very important, including the memorization and recitation of poetry. While her emphasis on music and art appreciation may not have made her theories especially unique in nineteenth-century Britain, they are today.

And her methods for teaching science have more in common with Charles Darwin's than your typical American high school curriculum. While parents are often impressed when high schools introduce the topics of neuroscience or quantum physics, Richard Louv points out that many schools have all but stopped teaching botany and zoology. But the powers of observation that are formed from going outside and studying our immediate surroundings more deeply cannot be replicated by delving into these other important, but much more abstract, topics.

Amy Snell is one of the founders of CMA. She used to teach in a local public high school but now devotes her time to the CMA and homeschooling her own four children—three girls and a boy under the age of eleven. For many of the parents who bring their kids here on Friday afternoon, it has not been an easy adjustment. "A lot of the moms didn't grow up in nature," says Snell. "We try to go out in all weather," which has bothered some of them. "There were moms who thought bugs were gross." But watching their kids swimming in the creek, holding boat races, building forts, and even tending to campfires has been eye opening, and even inspiring, for them.

In his book *How to Raise a Wild Child*, paleontologist Scott Sampson describes being a little kid, going on a walk with his mother a few blocks from their home. He started to go out into a frog pond. His boots were quickly flooded as he became fascinated by the tadpoles everywhere and moved farther out into the water. "I bent over and scooped up several with my hands to get a closer look. Bulging eyes, bloblike bodies, and long, slimy transparent tails worked madly against my fingers." Samspon adds parenthetically, "Many years later my mother told me that she started to object but thought better of it."[19]

It is hard as a mother to hold back those objections. Even if we are not worried about the dangers—maybe something will bite him, maybe he'll get sick from being wet and cold— we think about the mess we'll have to clean up and the extra laundry we'll have to do. It adds to our already long lists. What might have started out as a twenty-minute stroll around a lake has now become an hours-long project. Truth be told, it would have been much easier to be at home with an iPad app learning about tadpoles. But part of giving kids a greater sense of independence means holding back some objections.

Renee, a CMA mother who grew up in Ohio, recalls having much more freedom and access to nature as a child than her kids do. But the reason she started to homeschool her five kids was that she felt that they were so overscheduled they weren't getting enough "family time." She was excited about these Nature Club meetings because "I always wanted to go out and do more things outside with my kids, but somehow, with all the things to do at home, it didn't become a priority so we would stay home and make sure math was done and the house was clean, and other things were taken care of."

She found that "having the group made [spending time outside] a priority and made it fun, made it something we all looked forward to, especially being Friday afternoons. We would make sure we finished everything up then go outside for the afternoon." Cheryl Charles, who runs the Children and Nature Network, says that for parents, "there is safety and confidence in numbers." If other people are doing it, then it becomes something much more possible, and something parents will actually be more likely to commit to doing.

The goal of the group, according to Snell, has been not only to get the kids used to being in nature—after coming back to the same spot for five years it does start to feel very familiar and comfortable to them, like a second home—but also to get them used to unstructured play.

Snell is not exactly a free-range parent, as she tells me. She believes that there are plenty of things she doesn't want her kids exposed to yet, including a lot of popular culture and technology. But she also believes there is too much hovering over children when it comes to letting them discover things about their physical environments and in terms of their inter-actions with other children.

Snell believes in what she calls "masterly inactivity": "You are still setting boundaries and exercising oversight, but you are not being too much with your child." Parents, she says, "are the authority and you set up boundaries and then you are inactive and let kids have freedom." As much as possible the parents let the children work out any conflicts for themselves.

They do not try to separate the bigger kids from the littler ones or stop kids from doing anything that might involve a risk.

I was reminded of Snell's description when I was talking to a friend who lives in Washington, DC, and has two children under the age of three. She told me that when she gets home from work and has to prepare dinner for the kids by herself, she won't put them in front of the television or give them her phone to play with. Instead, she puts them inside of a gated area in the kitchen with some toys. She calls it "the circle of neglect."

As our kids get older and prepare themselves for life outside of our home, we want the circle of neglect to expand gradually. We want our boundaries to grow bigger and bigger, knowing that our kids have learned lessons from being confined to smaller boundaries and have proven themselves to be responsible adolescents and now young adults. This is necessary for them to grow up, but it's also important for the emotional well-being of parents. If you don't have a circle of neglect, you have to follow them around all day.

It's not easy to set boundaries, especially when it comes to technology. Snell has largely cut it out, but she tries "to replace it with something better." For one thing, her kids have a lot of freedoms—at the park and other places—that their friends might not. Her kids read a lot but they also explore a lot. And they have a group of friends with whom they can do the same. The oldest kids in the group are finishing high school now, and she says they are frustrated with the fact that their friends from outside the group "don't want to do anything. They just want to play video games."

Not every family in the group has eliminated screen time for their kids. "It would be naïve to think we could live without technology," says Snell. But many of the mothers have gotten rid of their phones or shut down their Facebook accounts. "Technology is a tool we can use but it doesn't control us now."

Like many of the kids I've met whose access to technology has been restricted either by their parents or their school or both, the kids in the park that day seemed less anxious, less "hurried." There is no way to say conclusively that their lack of access to technology is the direct cause of their temperament, but the two seem related. These kids, even the teenagers in the group, still seem able to view the world with a sense of child-like wonder. They are not jaded or bored, waiting impatiently to get to the next activity. Childhood, for them, is not simply, as David Elkind puts it, "the anteroom to adulthood."[20]

The confidence that both the parents and the kids exude in CMA comes in part from their numbers. Many parents have talked to me about how they always wanted to get their kids outside, to get them away from video games and phones, and they felt that CMA provided them with a community in which to do it. Parents can set wider boundaries, but if their kids are the only ones allowed to climb trees or walk to the park by themselves it won't matter much. Not only do kids enjoy exploring with other kids, but as we have seen in recent years, parents who allow their kids more independence are often shamed by others or even find themselves in jeopardy with law enforcement. You can't let your child walk to the playground alone if Child Services is going to pay you a visit as a result.

Boundaries are set by parents, but ideally they're agreed upon by communities. And that is where we are stuck today. There are many parents who want their children to achieve a certain kind of independence—a surefootedness not only in the forest but also in their daily social interactions. But it is hard to push that kind of independence without peers who are

*Tips for Cutting Back*

Community standards are not just set by other people. If you want to change the way that others near you think about how children should use their time, speak up—and not just with words. Instead of buying things that light up and make noise for birthday presents, have your kids pick out books for their friends.

being pushed in the same way. What Snell and other parents have determined is that when it comes to parenting, there is only so much you want to push against the culture and only so much that you can.

Similarly, and relatedly, there are boundaries that many families would like to set on the use of technology, but it is increasingly hard to do so when it seems as though other parents in the neighborhood, the schools, and the broader culture are all working at cross purposes. You can let your kids walk to the park by themselves and hang out in the neighborhood until the streetlights come on, but if all their friends are on a park bench watching YouTube videos on their phone, the effect is not what you are looking for.

On his blog at the *American Conservative*, Rod Dreher posted a letter from a reader in the spring of 2016: "I am 100 percent on board with your indictment of technology for kids," a mother writes. "How does a family, however, handle the isolation and loneliness that comes with being 'disconnected' from others?"[21] The reader explains that though she and her husband have flip phones, their four teenagers do not. They have computers in the family room but the websites they can access are limited.

She confesses: "The few people who still bother with us think we are nuts. We are social outcasts, and I really think it has to do with the technology thing. One by one, we have seen good families cave in and get iPads and smartphones for their kids. When we mention the serious problems with this, we get blank stares or they politely change the subject and soon distance themselves from us."

Ironically, these sentiments are not uncommon. Parents all over the country, from different religious communities and with kids of all ages at different kinds of schools, seem to feel as though they are parenting alone, in a kind of vacuum. We want our kids to be strong, independent, thoughtful, and able to resist the winds of culture. But we need at least a few allies in this effort.

In 2017, Tim Farnum, an anesthesiologist in Colorado, launched a campaign for a ballot measure that would make it illegal for retailers in his state to sell phones if the intended owner is younger than thirteen.[22] Farnum, who would need three hundred thousand signatures to get the measure on the 2018 ballot, received plenty of criticism—mostly from people saying this should be a matter for individual families to decide.

In principle, the critics are right. Still, Farnum's quixotic effort speaks to a problem many parents have faced. Even if they ban phones for their own children, other parents giving their kids phones can make life pretty difficult. None of us parent in a vacuum. When all of the other kids are making plans on their phones, will your child be an outcast if he or she doesn't have one? When you are carpooling with parents whose kids have cell phones but yours doesn't, will it cause logistical problems? Do you want your kid to be the odd man out? If you tell your kid to spend time outside playing but everyone else is at home on the iPad, your child will be the one without playmates.

*Tips for Cutting Back*

Keep your friends close and your enemies closer. There will be other parents who understand your rules for devices and those who do not. No, you can't monitor your kids' activities at other people's homes. But you can decide where your child should go and make clear to other parents what your rules are.

The paradox is that in order raise independent kids, many of us feel the need to severely restrict their access to culture in the first place. But if we control too much, if our circle of neglect is too small, don't we risk leaving them vulnerable when they are young adults?

Michele, the mother of two college students, tells me that her son didn't earn a single credit his first semester at an engineering school. She and her husband effectively lost twenty-five thousand dollars that fall. "He went to school and it was hard caring for himself." When he was home, she would tell him to do his laundry and make sure he ate his dinner. But at school, "there was no one checking in. He was staying up all night playing video games." She says he had not learned "how to self-regulate."

Michele compares her son's upbringing to her own. "I started getting that independence much earlier because our parents didn't micromanage us. They didn't know where we were." Today, she says, "it's hard for kids to mature outside of [their] parents' shadow." But she says parents have to figure out a way to make it happen. "We are who we are because of our parents. You may not like who your kids are, but that's your fault not theirs."

Perhaps this judgment sounds overly harsh, but the truth is this: as much as we have reason to fault the technology companies, our schools, other families, and even the broader culture for the choices our kids make with screens, parents are the bottom line. And it's time we start acting like it.

# Conclusion

■ ■ ■ ■

"I DEFINITELY PLAN TO give her more freedom. She's thirteen. If she could make all good decisions for herself already, she could move out." That was Kirsten, the mother of a teenage daughter in Washington, DC, who told me she severely limits her daughter's access to technology—no television or social media or cell phone, but a little *Minecraft* occasionally. Kirsten believes that the way she is bringing up her daughter is working. What's the evidence? Kirsten says her daughter recognizes that when she plays *Minecraft* for too long she doesn't read as much. And she likes reading.

Not surprisingly, many of the parents I spoke with say that teaching kids to self-regulate begins with the parent's sense of his or her own role. Linda, who is raising her eight- and five-year-old in what she describes as an affluent area of Charlotte, says that she has had to become confident in her own choices about the kids' habits. "You're the mom. You're in charge. When I say turn off the TV, we turn off the TV. I'm not worried about being their best friend or them not liking me. That argument doesn't have purchase with me."

But it gets harder. Maureen, who has five children between the ages of four and seventeen, remembers when her oldest daughter was in elementary school and she told her mother that all the other kids were wearing slip-on shoes to school, instead of Mary Janes. "Everyone wears slip-ons." Maureen even remembers the shoe salesman telling her the same thing. "A week or so later I'm volunteering at lunchtime on the playground. I see her shoes falling off. Everyone else but two kids are wearing Mary Janes." Maureen looks back laughing. "I fell for it and I'm sure I'll fall for it again. But I thought to take note for when she is a teenager."

Parents of multiple kids are often less likely to fall for it. They seem to care less about being their kid's friend. They seem to know that there will be ups and downs to the relationship with their children, that everyone else is not always doing what their kids say and that saying no to your child is not going to be the end of the world.

Elise, who has five children and has lived in both New York City and South Carolina with them, tells me that she thinks other parents are far too concerned about their kids' popularity. She doesn't want her kids to be outcasts, but "as long as they have a few friends" they'll be fine.

In holding the line against the culture, it helps to have a partner. Maureen tells me that "one of the biggest factors is for parents to make the joint decision that they're going to be countercultural. You have to make a firm decision to do that. So when the onslaught comes you have a shared mission."

Jamie and his wife both grew up on a lot of television—a television in every room, dinnertime viewing, and so forth. When they started dating, they had both moved away from TV, deciding that there were other things they wanted to do with their time. But having kids cemented that view in their minds. And they have extended it to restricting access to all screens.

The two have found it important to maintain a united front, particularly since their respective families find their choices strange. "They would give us a hard time about the fact we weren't letting [their older daughter] watch TV."

The single parents I interviewed had things much harder. Not only were they solely responsible for helping kids find an alternative to technology, but they were often battling with their former partners over a technology policy. One mother told me that her ex-husband gave the kids much more screen time than she did, not only undermining her goals but also making her kids enjoy spending time at their dad's house more.

It is not only divorced and blended families that have more tension on this issue. When I first started interviewing people on this topic, I was surprised by the difficulty that extended family seemed to create for enforcing rules about technology. But in some ways it is perfectly predictable. Parents regularly disagree with grandparents and aunts and uncles about what's best for children. When extended families are in close quarters for prolonged periods of time—as in vacations and holiday celebrations—conflicts inevitably arise.

That being said, many parents did report that having extended family nearby was often a great help in creating the kind of atmosphere they wanted for their children. Susan, the mother of two teenage girls and one eleven-year-old boy, reported that her daughters' relationship with their cousins, who lived nearby and were similar ages, allowed the girls to extend childhood a little longer. While their friends may have been taking sexy selfies, her daughters and their cousins often asked to roast marshmallows and play on the tire swing in the backyard. Perhaps this sounds idyllic, but Maureen insists she did not force her kids into this 1950s vision of childhood. Rather, she suggests that having extended family nearby gave them a kind of safe space in which to continue to be kids for a few more years. Even when our nuclear families have shrunk, living near extended families can provide the kind of available playmates that make screens seem more superfluous.

Punita and her husband are from India. Before moving to Madison, Wisconsin, for her husband's job, Punita was living with her husband's parents, brother, sister, and their children. While she acknowledges it can be a challenge having so many people under one roof, "it helps in bringing up kids." Children had more playmates around. There were more adults around to supervise when necessary and, as a result, the children had more freedom. Knowing that adults would always be nearby also meant that the kids' lives didn't need to be as strictly scheduled.

Now Punita says she feels like she needs to sign her kids up for activities all the time, lest they want to play video games or watch television every afternoon. It is true that one method for dealing with too much screen time is to schedule a lot of extracurricular activities. If your child is practicing on the swim team for two hours every afternoon in addition to doing homework and editing the school newspaper, the chances of wasting time on Snapchat are significantly diminished, but there are downsides to this approach as well.

Too many time commitments after school seem to ensure that kids don't get to experiment with freedom while they are growing up. And when they leave for college or life in the real world, it may be harder for them to know what to do with unstructured time.

So what are the other options? When I talked to Erica, a mother of two in New Jersey, she told me that she was very impressed by her neighbor's kids. The daughter did some babysitting for her. And she found herself consulting this other mother for advice. She wanted to know the "secret sauce."

Psychologist Wendy Mogel says this is the right approach. "I always encourage parents—even though things are changing quickly—to find parents with kids a little older who are turning out nicely." That phrase—turning out nicely—is so quaint. It's obviously a judgment call, but I think it sums up the reaction I had to the kids at CMA. They were turning out nicely. I can't predict for sure they won't become juvenile delinquents, but I have a pretty good hunch.

## Tips for Cutting Back

Find allies. If you're the kind of parent who doesn't care what other parents think or do, good for you. If you're not, find friends who are also concerned about their kids' exposure to technology. Nurture those friendships.

Erica's neighbor Joan is the woman with the kids who were turning out nicely. Her daughter and son are both in their early twenties now. And she says her sauce was not much of a secret. Her kids were very active with sports and music. They attended church regularly and were involved in their community. And they went to a school that discouraged the use of too much technology. Now her son, who is twenty-two, is about to purchase a "non-smart phone." His mother reports that he has better ways to spend his money than on a data plan and he wanted to get away from the distractions, too.

Thinking back to their childhood, Joan says she "encouraged them to get involved in things that would help them with their life rather than things that are a waste of time." They weren't going to become professional athletes or musicians, but they were good enough. And Joan also tried to help them develop ways to regulate themselves. "You have to be able to calm yourself down," she says. Technology, she believes, is not the way to do that.

In his book *The Shallows*, Nicholas Carr says that he had to turn off his email so he could let his brain "breathe" again.[1] Other authors have reported similar experiences. In 2015, Alan Jacobs, a professor and blogger who was very active on social media, explained why he was quitting Twitter, getting a dumb phone, and starting to write in a journal rather than on his computer. Now when he is at the coffee shop, he explains: "If my mind wanders and I wonder what's in my RSS feed, I can't check, so I have to go back to writing. Sometimes I bring a book too, and read it. If I get tired of it, I don't have anything else to read, so I either keep going anyway or get the notebook back out. Or just sit there and drink my coffee and watch the unphotographed world go by."[2]

Because Carr and Jacobs are intelligent adults, they know what is making it hard for them to think and work. They know what causes them anxiety too. But our teenagers do not. We have to teach them how to calm themselves down.

Many of the parents I interviewed said they had tried to introduce particular no-technology times of the day or times of the week. No phones at the dinner table, for example. Parents often report that they violate it themselves when work is calling. They feel guilty about this and worry that they are setting a bad example for their children. As with so many parenting decisions, the concern about hypocrisy often gets in the way of parents making the right choices. Even if you smoked pot as a teenager, you can still tell your kids it's a terrible idea. Set a rule about when phones are allowed. If you violate it once in a while, so what? You can tell your kids that you're the grown-up.

In every household, there are different rules for children and adults. And there's no reason why the use of technology should be any different. For one thing, adults are fully formed people. While, as Carr points out, our brains are still malleable even as we grow older and technology can change the way we think and work, it is also true that we have come to understand the enjoyment of reading or walking outside or having a face-to-face conversation. And our advanced age makes us more skeptical of the value of taking hundreds of selfies each week.

*Tips for Cutting Back*

It's okay to be a hypocrite. Yes, we can all use a little less time on our screens—adults included—but stop thinking that the rules have to be the same for you and your kids. You don't give your kids alcohol or the keys to the car. Why should they have the same access to devices as you?

If you really are just playing on Facebook, put the phone down. But if you have to answer work emails, don't beat yourself up.

• • • •

What about an entire day without technology? Since 2010, tens of thousands of people have participated in the National Day of Unplugging. A group called Reboot, a hip Jewish non-profit, has encouraged Jews to unplug from their devices each Sabbath. Observant Jews don't use electricity on the Sabbath and so they generally don't use their phones or computers. But even less traditionally minded Jews have started to adopt this practice (plenty of non-Jews have also stumbled onto this idea). While they may not go to synagogue or refrain from other activities prohibited by Jewish law, they'll gladly turn off their phones for a day.

Liz says she started tech-free Sundays about a year ago.

"We go to church and get things done around the house and go out and do something as a family." But she says that she and her husband "have to plan things" to keep her son and daughter (ages nine and eleven) "busy" on those days. It's "hard to do when technology is self gratifying." Actually, this is an argument against just having a one-day-off rule. Kids get so used to using screens for hours on end the rest of the week that it becomes that much harder to readjust to life without them on that tech Sabbath. One advantage of a religious Sabbath over a self-imposed one is that a higher power is holding you to it.

Some parents are less consistent about giving their kids time away from technology. Guy, the father of three in Cleveland, sometimes takes away his kids' phones and devices as punishment. Or he just thinks they've been on them too much. Regardless, he finds that initially there is a great amount of complaining, but after a few days of no video games, they get used to it. "I find once they are unplugged from the device, they don't miss it. I forget to give it back and they forget to ask."

It's a reminder that even older kids can adjust pretty quickly. It may seem like a family culture is set in stone—like watching television every night or allowing our kids to play on phones when we're in line at the supermarket—but it is perfectly possible to wake up tomorrow and make a different set of rules if you decided it would improve your kids' lives or your family's time together. As with most aspects of parenting, though, consistency makes things easier. If you want your kids to stop begging for your phone in the car or at the soccer field, you pretty much have to always say no.

We changed our screen policy a few years ago. The transformation didn't occur overnight. Shortly after our son started first grade, we decided to eliminate technology on weekdays.

It was a difficult transition, especially for our oldest daughter, who had been watching a little television before bed since she was a few months old. But the results were encouraging. Evenings seemed less rushed, less stressful. There was no arguing over what to watch or how long to watch it. The kids read instead, or played board games with each other. Time really did go by more slowly, but not in a bad way.

Now the older ones have homework and other activities, which means that we play games with our youngest or read to her. It was frankly easier to put on a cartoon to keep her busy while the others needed our attention, but it was not a habit I wanted to have to break. Now no one asks for screens during the week—even on most holidays—because the expectation is that they're not available.

For some families, the rule about technology is that it comes last. Renee, the mother of five who takes her kids to CMA, says, "I intentionally make sure they have time—unscheduled time—every day, where they don't have any requirements. They can be on their own or with each other. They can be inside or outside."

Other parents tell me that if their child has read, played outside, done schoolwork, and spent time with family they are happy to hand over a device if there are still a few minutes at the end of the day. But every other box has to be checked off first. This plan echoes the AAP guidelines—which recommend school, homework, an hour of physical activity, social interaction, and eight to twelve hours of sleep. Only then should screens be made available.

As Jamie explains, it's not that there is no reason to use technology. It's that "I want them to prioritize human interaction." As Renee explains about her oldest son, "he knows how to use technology, but also how to turn it off and what else is available."

One way of getting across to kids the social costs of spending too much time on a screen is by imposing some financial costs on them. One father I spoke with said that he required his kids to complete a set of chores before he would give them that week's Wi-Fi code at their home. Others make their children pay for any data plan they use. A number of parents remarked on the absurd expenses of keeping everyone in a family connected. But even in families that can well afford these bills, there is a good reason to make kids aware of the cost because when they leave home they will be bearing them on their own.

In 2015, Jared Cramer, a father in Virginia, made national news when he decided that he was going to lock his thirteen-year-old daughter out of her own closet until she paid him back the $541 in cell phone charges she racked up in a single month.[3] By doing chores around the house, Julia, whom news outlets reported was an otherwise good student and a kind person, planned eventually to regain access to her clothes and accessories. Nevertheless, it was a little shocking that her father didn't notice she was on the phone enough to rack up those charges. Some might say that the time lost using that data is more valuable than the money.

The reason that Susan limits her kids' technology use has nothing to do with money, and it's not even a "moral argument," she says. Rather, she thinks that there are better ways for them to spend their time. When they're young that means being outside more, playing with friends. "If you're child is spending time on devices when they're little, you're taking their childhood away."

As they get older, Susan believes there are all sorts of other things they should be studying and reading and doing to develop their minds and bodies. "We are not going to spend our lives being passive consumers." Now that her oldest child is fourteen, though, she does not seem particularly worried that when he leaves home he will go crazy consuming media. By that point, she says, "They have looked critically at media and they have found other ways of spending time. They see the benefit of not being super plugged in."

Waiting longer to give kids access to technology is not merely a matter of expanding boundaries slowly and then seeing if they can be trusted. It's also a matter of developing their tastes and temperaments. It's a matter of exposing them to all the other things in the world besides technology that they might enjoy and that might make them more thoughtful and even happier people. It's like those teenagers who decide not to use drugs because they are so consumed by sports. It's not that getting high with friends doesn't look fun. It's that they love something else more.

The temptations of technology are enormous at every stage of life. When we have young children, technology is a distraction. But it is easy to see how this desire for distraction can extend far beyond toddlerhood.

Jim Holt, when reviewing a book called *Faster: The Acceleration of Just About Everything* by James Gleick, asks an important question: "Why is it that, whenever humans are given the choice, we opt for faster?" Holt offers this observation from nineteenth-century aphorist Sir Arthur Helps: "Almost all human affairs are tedious. Everything is too long. Visits, dinners, concerts, plays, speeches, pleadings, essays, sermons are too long." Holt concludes: "Our connivance in the acceleration of just about everything, in short, may arise from our capacity to be bored by just about anything."

But people—and especially children—have the opposite capacity as well. To be interested in just about anything. From slimy tadpoles, the view from the car window, silly conversations with siblings, books on obscure topics, or the musings of their own minds, our kids can be awed by things we adults have not considered interesting in some time. Parents like to talk about how their kids prefer to play with the wrapping paper sometimes instead of the present inside or the pots and pans instead of the expensive age-appropriate toys we purchase. Sometimes we just don't wait long enough for them to find something to do, something that will engage them. Like Scott Sampson's mother, we need to hold back a little longer to let our children explore.

But we also need to remember to be awed by them. When I spoke to Peter Whybrow, the neuroscientist at University of California Los Angeles, he told me he was concerned with all of these parents who wanted to give their kids technology so they could go get something else done. "You learn quite a lot from children. Your presence within their realm is so much more important than fobbing them off so you can go read your book or play on your phone." Whybrow is puzzled about why pediatricians don't offer stronger counsel on screen time. "They're not interested in saying, 'Get to know your kid. You'll find this person is really quite fascinating.'" But "this," says Whybrow, "is the beginning of character."

The childhood virtues of spontaneity, purity, strength, and joy, which Rousseau saw as natural to our young selves, are getting harder for our sons and daughters to recapture. We assume that they are as jaded as we are, that they are going to recoil in boredom and annoyance as soon as they are left to their own devices, instead of their own "devices."

If it is true, as Neil Postman writes, that audiences are "captivated by variety and repelled by complexity," who is to blame?[4] At least in part it is us—the parents for acculturating our children to the former while shielding them from the latter. How do we let our kids get a little bored, a little more willing to daydream, to think for a longer period of time about something, without rushing to offer them something else to do?

Our desire to cater to our children's desire for more entertainment did not spring from nowhere. There are companies, schools, and a whole culture that are using our anxieties against us. There are people trying to sell us more screens and more apps and more programs to entertain them. Indeed, the games themselves are designed to get us to want to play more.

You don't have to be addicted to slot machines in Vegas in order to be a victim of this technology. Can we expect our kids to moderate their behavior when the programs we give them are designed to make us use them immoderately?

And what about the worlds created by these games? Maybe *Minecraft* and *Sim City* encourage some creativity on the part of kids—though there's no evidence it's more than the creativity encouraged by a set of blocks or Legos—but the vast majority of the games are the kind where nothing surprising can happen.

Then there are schools trying to persuade us that technology will teach our kids more, better and faster. The temptation of technology for parents of schoolchildren is clear. We want them to have all the advantages, to know more than their peers, to be one step ahead when it comes to math or reading. We are looking for apps and programs that will help them get into the right high school, the right college, and the right job when they finish. It is hard for parents to separate the great uses of technology in the classroom—like more differentiated learning—from all the bells and whistles that seem like they will make our children more knowledgeable but probably won't.

There are so few voices saying that human interaction needs to be the priority, that the ability to communicate face-to-face with other people is an important lesson. There are so few voices saying that the skills children need for jobs will still be reading and writing and doing math and thinking broadly and deeply, that using computers is something you can always learn later. Indeed, the programs are made so that a three-year-old can figure them out.

Moreover, the way we learn from our screens, whether watching television or reading websites or viewing online videos, it's all contributing to our "peek-a-boo" world. Snippets of information come into view, but not for long enough that we would actually take the time and effort to examine their veracity. And then they just disappear again. We absorb so little of what we take in online because websites are designed for distraction. Our kids have not had the time to learn slowly and deeply before we drop them into this ocean of information that will only wash over them.

And there is the culture. It is a culture that celebrates technology, not only because it has brought us a world of knowledge at our fingertips or because it has made every part of our lives more convenient. But it celebrates technology because technology allows us access to everything and everyone right now. It is a culture that values anything happening this minute over anything that happened yesterday or last year or in the last century. This is one of the reasons our teenagers love technology. It means that a seventeen-year-old can go head-to-head with a fifty-year-old and win. Because the former is just as likely to know what happened five minutes ago.

There are many reasons adolescents like technology. As Sherry Turkle points out, on the Internet, people can "cycle through" many selves.[5] Virtual communities offer people permission to experiment. But that too is a double-edged sword. Giving kids permission to experiment is another way of saying that we won't hold them accountable for the things they say and do online. But, if anything, technology has succeeded in making it more difficult and even dangerous for teens to experiment. It has made the silliness of adolescence into something that is potentially permanently damaging.

Though the Internet may seem like a way for people to experiment, to venture outside of their traditional boundaries of family and community, it has actually served to make young people more risk averse. When Gardner and Davis interviewed camp directors about their experiences with kids, they found that "campers today demonstrate more self-confidence in what they say they can do but are less willing to test their abilities through action."[6] Those interviewed "attributed this shift to youth's growing distaste for taking any tangible risk that could end in failure—failure that once might have been witnessed by a few peers and then forgotten but today might become a part of one's permanent digital footprint."[7]

How can we help children to function freely and independently when they are always tethered to a device? They can never be out of touch. Which means that whenever they need to make a decision of even the slightest import, they can always consult a parent. And they often do.

Marie Winn wrote that television returns children to a "state of helplessness."[8] But all of the screens that have come into our lives in the forty years since she wrote that have made the problem much worse. Kids rely on devices for entertainment, for school, for communication, for self-esteem, for socialization, for direction, and for distraction.

Shortly before I finished this manuscript, I sent my nine-year-old daughter off to a month of sleepover camp a couple of hours away from home. Like many such institutions, the camp does not allow the kids to have any sort of screen with them—no phones, no digital cameras, no tablets.

It is remarkable that so many parents who have bought their children phones and give them plenty of access to tablets and computers during the rest of the year would happily send their child away for a month or two to a place with no technology. It implies that many parents really do think that their kids need a break. It implies that as much as parents are happy to hand over screens at home, they would prefer not to.

If someone could wave a magic wand and ensure that their kids are being entertained and educated without screens, that would be even better. There is clearly a critical mass of parents who see iPads and phones and social media as problematic influences on our children's lives. While they are not willing to parent against the culture for most of the year, they would happily go low tech if that's what their kids wanted to do for the summer—if that's what other kids were doing.

But why not the rest of the year? And why are we waiting for a magic wand? We already have one in our hands. We can't control what every other child has access to, but we can surely exert more influence over our own families.

### *Tips for Cutting Back*

Diets are diets, whether they're for food or screen time. If you're not consistent in the first few weeks about the rules, you will fail. Kids will sense your weakness and they will keep asking until you break down.

In a way, despite the fact that sleepover camp is a fairly common choice in our community, this is the first month in a long time that Emily's life will look like everyone else's. No one will have phones. No one will watch videos or play games online. No one will be taking selfies or texting. Everyone will be enjoying the outside or reading books or playing cards.

It has been strange to think about what my daughter is doing during this time away. We can send each other letters back and forth, but I won't find out what's going on until four or five days after it happens. While she is in a protected environment, she will be making choices about what to eat, what to wear, how to communicate with other people, whom to talk to if something is bothering her—all without being able to consult me. And the stories she constructs in her letters will be what she wants to tell me, not what one of her friends has posted on Instagram.

A month of camp is a very expensive way to keep a child in a technology-free environment. And certainly that wasn't the only reason we chose to send her. But there are clearly plenty of other parents willing to pay for this luxury. There are so few spaces left where kids can be left alone, where we (and other parents) cannot hover. It is not because I am nostalgic, or even because I am a Luddite, that I think a month without screens is a good idea. It's because children without technology are more independent, more confident, and more free.

It is possible to re-create this kind of freedom with a supportive spouse, with an extended family that agrees with you, in a neighborhood or religious community where other adults support your goals. No matter what your income level, giving a child independence from technology is within reach if you have those supports.

But what if you're not part of a community that shares your values? Then you have a bigger problem. But I have become convinced during the course of the research for this book that there are more parents out there than you think who want

these same things for their children. Finding them may not
be easy, but it is not impossible. And it is an important step
in bringing up a happy, well-adjusted child.

In an essay by Michael Chabon called "Manhood for Amateurs," the novelist writes:

> Childhood is, or has been, or ought to be, the great
> original adventure, a tale of privation, courage, con-
> stant vigilance, danger, and sometimes calamity.
> For the most part the young adventurer sets forth
> equipped only with the fragmentary map—marked
> HERE THERE BE TYGERS and MEAN KID WITH AIR
> RIFLE—that he or she has been able to construct
> out of a patchwork of personal misfortune, bed-
> time reading, and the accumulated local lore of the
> neighborhood children.[9]

As parents, it is our job to give kids the map. We need to give
them the tools to see the boundaries, to understand the legend, to use the compass. Chabon laments:

> The thing that strikes me now when I think about
> the Wilderness of Childhood is the incredible degree
> of freedom my parents gave me to adventure there.
> A very grave, very significant shift in our idea of
> childhood has occurred since then. The Wilderness
> of Childhood is gone; the days of adventure are past.
> The land ruled by children, to which a kid might
> exile himself for at least some portion of every day
> from the neighboring kingdom of adulthood, has in
> large part been taken over, co-opted, colonized, and
> finally absorbed by the neighbors.[10]

In place of the Wilderness of Childhood, we have given our kids the World of Devices. But who are we kidding? These screens are the markers of adulthood. Kids may find them entertaining. They can use them to pretend to be grown-up. They can sit quietly and text their friends, just like mom and dad do. But there is no adventure to be had with them. And so our kids miss the great trials and triumphs of childhood and remain unprepared for the great difficulties and joys of adulthood.

# The Tech-lash

■ ■ ■ ■ ■

THE YEAR 2018 seems to have marked the beginning of the "tech-lash," when ordinary Americans finally began to realize the price of our love affair with Silicon Valley. Sure, there were mea culpas that had started to trickle out from tech gurus about the harms of social media on our families. "God only knows what it's doing to our children's brains," Sean Parker, founding president of Facebook, announced in 2017. Chamath Palihapitiya, the company's former vice president for user growth, noted more bluntly that he doesn't let his kids use "this shit."

But it was in 2018 that Mark Zuckerberg himself sat down in front of Congress to answer some important questions. And slowly it became clear not only to our political leaders, but also to the mothers and fathers watching these exchanges, that something was amiss. Senator Richard J. Durbin, Democrat of Illinois, asked Zuckerberg whether he would be comfortable sharing the name of the hotel he stayed in last night or if he would be comfortable sharing the names of the people he had messaged this week.

"No. I would probably not choose to do that publicly here," Zuckerberg responded.

"I think that may be what this is all about," Durbin said. "Your right to privacy. The limits of your right to privacy. And how much you give away in modern America in the name of, quote, connecting people around the world."

In the aftermath of this exchange and the revelations about how the firm Cambridge Analytica not only targeted particular people with their ads on Facebook but also used "psychographic analysis" to figure out exactly what kinds of prompts would push users to vote a certain way, a number of adults confessed to me their surprise. Slightly embarrassed, they told me they didn't realize the ways in which social media companies were using their personal information not only to make a profit but also to change their behavior.

It would be easy for me to say: "What took you so long?" Eighteen years ago, a friend was shocked to find that voicemails from his first lost cell phone would simply pop up magically on his new one. I don't mean to sound paranoid but there is lots of information out there about us. And, "in the name of, quote, connecting" to other people around the world we are sharing more every day. Thanks to so many proud parents who want to tell the world about their children's triumphs and foibles, there is a ton of information about our kids online as well.

Perhaps it is time for our own mea culpa as parents. We have not been mindful about the way we engage with technology in our own lives and we have set a terrible example for our children. We have not given our children proper guidance about how to use technology in their own lives, and in our rush to keep our kids occupied or entertained or ahead of their peers, we have given up too much of their childhoods to screens.

Much damage has been done to our families by the use of phones and tablets and laptops and even televisions. But it is never too late to rethink the role of these devices in our homes and our classrooms—not to mention everywhere else we bring them.

In the year since *Be the Parent, Please* was first published,

I have spent a number of evenings in schools and houses of worship discussing its implications with parents. Some of these mothers and fathers have focused on the practical questions. They ask me: "At what age should I give my child a cell phone?" "How many hours should my child play *Fortnite*?" "What if all his friends are on it?"

Others parents wanted to probe deeper into the research on exactly what harm too much time on these devices can cause. The people who came to these events were mostly mothers. The fathers who did attend were more skeptical of attempts to restrict technology for their children. It didn't harm *them* to be playing video games growing up. How would it hurt their children? They conceded that pornography had changed— both the content and the easy access. And they were worried about their daughters being subject to harassment and bullying on social media.

It is not only parents who are starting to have second (or third, or fourth) thoughts about the way their kids use screens. The kids are too. According to a Pew Survey from August 2018, 54 percent of teens say they spend too much time on their cell phone and 41 percent[1] say they spend too much time on social media. They are even conscious enough of the problem that many have tried to cut back. More than half have said they have tried to reduce their cell phone use, their time on social media, and the hours spent playing video games. More than half of teens "associate the absence of their cell phone with at least one of these three emotions: loneliness, being upset, or feeling anxious."[2]

It is a sign of progress that they are recognizing these feelings. But despite these pleas for help, only 57 percent of parents report setting any restrictions on their kids' screen time. And one reason for that is that parents struggle with their own use of technology—36 percent[3] say they themselves spend too much time on their cellphone. And it's not just their impression: 51 percent of teens "say they often or sometimes find their parent or caregiver to be distracted by their own cellphone when they are trying to have a conversation with them."[4]

Ultimately, and happily from my perspective, these evening meeting with parents turned into forums for them to start to figure out what role technology should have in their families and in their communities. Parents remarked to me that they saw other mothers and fathers at these events they weren't expecting, people they didn't think were concerned about the use of technology. Some parents were worried that their kids were victims of poor treatment online. While others acknowledged that their children didn't always exercise the best judgment when figuring out how to treat their peers.

The premise of *Be the Parent, Please* was that none of us can raise a family in a vacuum. And even if we could, it would make our lives immeasurably harder and our children's lives less enjoyable if we didn't have peers who shared our values. These evenings confirmed for me that there are a few, if not dozens, of parents in each community who are concerned about technology use and who are looking for ways to reclaim childhood for their families.

For those parents who believe it's time to cut back on screen time—to limit the number of hours a day and the number of days a week that their kids are on screens—and replace those hours with time spent outside or playing board games or reading or sharing meals with their families, I hope that this book can provide some useful information and strategies for accomplishing these goals.

But I also hope that this book can spark a conversation with other families. The following questions are inspired by some of the discussions I have had with parents this year. I am grateful for their hospitality, and I hope that their communities can serve as a model for others going forward.

- What are the reasons that I give my children access to technology? Is it more for me or for them?
- What kinds of activities can we as a family substitute for screen use? What did I do when I was their age for fun? Are any of those activities possible? Would they enjoy them?
- Are my children spending as much time as they should outdoors? Are they able to go long periods of time without being distracted by texts or social media?
- Are my children able to complete homework without constantly checking email, texts, or social media updates?
- How do my children seem after they have engaged with friends on social media or group texts?
- Has technology become a crutch for my child? Is he or she less likely to make decisions independently or am I using technology as a means to tether them to me and make them less likely to interact with others?
- If I wanted to reduce the amount of screen time for my children, what would be the easiest place to start? Could we as a family pick one day of the week to be screen free or shrink the number of hours that screens are available to them each day?
- Are my spouse and I on the same page about screen time? Are the rules clear about phones at the dinner table or in the car?
- Am I bringing my children into settings that are meant for adults or older kids knowing that I can distract them with screens?
- Do I know other parents who are worried about their kids' use of technology? Could we try to form a "Wait

Until Eighth" group at our school or at least have some kind of informal meeting to talk about the tech questions in our community?

- Am I doing enough to keep up monitoring my children's electronic communications? Am I prepared to do more if I get them their own phone/tablet/laptop?
- Have I made clear to my children that I am monitoring their devices and that the use of devices is something that can be taken away at any point?
- Why do my kids use technology at school? Has the administration explained to parents the rationale for use of tablets during school hours or for homework? Can I press school officials for more information?

# Notes

....

INTRODUCTION

1. Jingjing Jiang, "How Teens and Parents Navigate Screen Time and Device Distractions," Pew Research Center, August 22, 2018, http://www.pewinternet.org/2018/08/22/how-teens-and-parents-navigate-screen-time-and-device-distractions/.
2. Ibid.
3. Ibid.
4. Ibbid

CHAPTER 1

1. "The Common Sense Census: Media Use by Tweens and Teens," Common Sense Media, November 3, 2015, https://www.common sensemedia.org/research/the-common-sense-census-media-use-by-tweens-and-teens.
2. "Generation M²: Media in the Lives of 8- to 18-Year-Olds," Kaiser Family Foundation, January 2010, https://kaiserfamilyfoundation.files.wordpress.com/2013/04/8010.pdf.
3. Ibid.
4. https://twitter.com/lvanderkam/status/838736552616415232.
5. American Academy of Pediatrics, "Media Use in School-Aged Children and Adolescents," *Pediatrics* (October 2016), http://pediatrics.aappublications.org/content/early/2016/10/19/peds.2016-2592.
6. Hailey Middlebrook, "New Screen Time Rules for Kids, by Doctors," CNN, October 21, 2016, http://www.cnn.com/2016/10/21/health/screen-time-media-rules-children-aap/index.html.
7. H. L. Kirkorian, T. A. Pempek, L. A. Murphy, M. E. Schmidt, and D. R. Anderson, "The Impact of Background Television on Parent–Child Interaction," *Child Development* 80 (2009): 1350–59, doi:10.1111/j.1467-8624.2009.01337.x.
8. L. D. Eron, L. R. Huesmann, M. M. Lefkowitz, and L. O. Walker, "Does Television Cause Aggression?" *American Psychologist* 27 (1972): 253–63.

9. L. R. Huesmann, J. Moise-Titus, C. Podolski, and L. D. Eron, "Longitudinal Relations between Children's Exposure to TV Violence and Their Aggressive and Violent Behavior in Young Adulthood: 1977–1992," *Developmental Psychology* 39 (2003): 2001–21.

10. C. A. Anderson, A. Shibuya, N. Ihori, E. L. Swing, B. J. Bushman, A. Sakamoto, H. R. Rothstein, and M. Saleem, "Violent Video Game Effects on Aggression, Empathy, and Prosocial Behavior in Eastern and Western Countries: A Meta-Analytic Review," *Psychological Bulletin* 136, no. 2 (2010): 151–73.

11. Alisha M. Crawley, Daniel R. Anderson, Alice Wilder, Marsha Williams, Angela Santomero, "Effects of Repeated Exposures to a Single Episode of the Television Program Blue's Clues on the Viewing Behaviors and Comprehension of Preschool Children," *Journal of Educational Psychology* 91, no. 4 (December 1999), 630–37, http://dx.doi.org/10.1037/0022-0663.91.4.630

12. Melissa S. Kearney and Phillip B. Levine, "Early Childhood Education by MOOC: Lessons from Sesame Street" (working paper, National Bureau of Economic Research, Cambridge, MA, 2015), http://www.nber.org/papers/w21229.

13. Eric E. Rasmussen, Autumn Shafer, Malinda J. Colwell, Shawna White, Narissra Punyanunt-Carter, Rebecca L. Densley, and Holly Wright, "Relation between Active Mediation, Exposure to *Daniel Tiger's Neighborhood*, and US Preschoolers' Social and Emotional Development," *Journal of Children and Media* 10, no. 4 (2016).

14. Ibid.

15. D. H. Uttal, N. G. Meadow, E. Tipton, L. L. Hand, A. R. Alden, C. Warren, and N. S. Newcombe, "The Malleability of Spatial Skills: A Meta-Analysis of Training Studies," Psychological Bulletin 139, no. 2 (2013): 352–402, doi:10.1037/a0028446.

16. B. T. McDaniel and J. S. Radesky, "Technoference: Parent Distraction With Technology and Associations With Child Behavior Problems," *Child Development* (2017), doi:10.1111/cdev.12822.

17. Jenny S. Radesky, Caroline J. Kistin, Barry Zuckerman, Katie Nitzberg, Jamie Gross, Margot Kaplan-Sanoff, Marilyn Augustyn, Michael Silverstein, "Patterns of Mobile Device Use by Caregivers and Children During Meals in Fast Food Restaurants," *Pediatrics* (March 2014), doi:10.1542/peds.2013-3703.

18. Kay S. Hymowitz, *Ready or Not: Why Treating Children as Small Adults Endangers Their Future—and Ours* (New York: Free Press, 1999).

19. Jennifer Senior, *All Joy and No Fun: The Paradox of Modern Parenthood* (New York: Ecco, 2015), 10.

20. Ibid.

21. Ron Lieber, *The Opposite of Spoiled: Raising Kids Who Are Grounded, Generous, and Smart About Money* (New York: Harper Paperbacks, 2016).

22. Amanda Kolson Hurley, "No, Your Kid May Not Have a Snack," *Washington Post*, May 28, 2015, https://www.washingtonpost.com /posteverything/wp/2015/05/28/no-you-cant-have-a-snack /?utm_term=.2399dcc336e8.

23. David Finkelhor, Anne Shattuck, Heather A. Turner, and Sherry L. Hamby, "Trends in Children's Exposure to Violence, 2003 to 2011," *JAMA Pediatrics* (2014), http://www.unh.edu/ccrc/pdf /poi130100.pdf.

## Chapter 2

1. Tamar Lewin, "No Einstein in Your Crib? Get a Refund," *New York Times*, October 23, 2009, http://www.nytimes.com/2009/10/24/edu cation/24baby.html.

2. Tamar Lewin, "A Growing Number of Video Viewers Watch from Crib," *New York Times*, October 29, 2003, http://www.nytimes. com/2003/10/29/us/a-growing-number-of-video-viewers-watch -from-crib.html.

3. Ibid.

4. J. M. Zosh, B. N. Verdine, A. Filipowicz, R. M. Golinkoff, K. Hirsh-Pasek, and N. S. Newcombe, "Talking Shape: Parental Language With Electronic Versus Traditional Shape Sorters," *Mind, Brain, and Education* 9 (2015): 136–44, doi:10.1111/mbe.12082.

5. Kathy Hirsh-Pasek, Jennifer M. Zosh, and Roberta Michnick Golinkoff, "Don't Let the Toys Do the Talking: The Case of Electronic and Traditional Shape Sorters," Brookings, September 8, 2015, https://www.brookings.edu/blog/education-plus-develop ment/2015/09/08/dont-let-the-toys-do-the-talking-the-case-of-elec tronic-and-traditional-shape-sorters/.

6. Melissa S. Kearney and Phillip B. Levine, "Early Childhood Education by MOOC: Lessons from Sesame Street" (working paper, National Bureau of Economic Research, Cambridge, MA, 2015), http://www.nber.org/papers/w21229.

7. Ibid.

8. Alia Wong. "The Sesame Street Effect," *Atlantic*, June 17, 2015, https://www.theatlantic.com/education/archive/2015/06/sesame -street-preschool-education/396056/.

9. Thomas D. Cook, Hilary Appleton, Ross F. Conner, Ann Shaffer,

Gary Tamkin, and Stephen J. Weber, *Sesame Street Revisited* (New York: Russell Sage Foundation, 1975), www.jstor.org/stable/10.775 8/9781610448277.

10. Ibid.

11. Ibid.

12. Malcolm Gladwell, *The Tipping Point: How Little Things Can Make a Big Difference* (London: Abacus, 2015).

13. Heather L. Kirkorian, Ellen A. Wartella, and Daniel R. Anderson, "Media and Children's Learning," *Future of Children* 18, no. 1 (2008): 39–61, https://www.princeton.edu/futureofchildren/publi cations/docs/18_01_03.pdf.

14. Ibid.

15. Dimitri A. Christakis, Frederick J. Zimmerman, David L. DiGiuseppe, and Carolyn A. McCarty, "Early Television Exposure and Subsequent Attentional Problems in Children," *Pediatrics* 113, no. 4 (2004): 708–13, doi:10.1542/peds.113.4.708.

16. Ibid.

17. Jane M. Healy, "Early Subsequent Exposure and Subsequent Attention Problems in Children," *Pediatrics* (2004), https://www.seattle-childrens.org/pdf/jane_healy_commentary.pdf.

18. Neil Postman, *Disappearance of Childhood* (New York: Random House, 1994), 79.

19. Ibid.

20. David Elkind, *The Hurried Child: Growing Up Too Fast Too Soon* (Boston: MA, Da Capo Press, 2009) xi.

21. Cheyenne MacDonald, "Bizarre Babypod 'Tampon Speaker' Can Play Music to Unborn Children," *Daily Mail*, January 5, 2016, http://www.dailymail.co.uk/sciencetech/article-3386181/Bizarre -babypod-tampon-speaker-play-music-unborn-children.html.

22. David Elkind, *The Hurried Child*, 104–5.

23. "Zero to Eight: Children's Media Use in America 2013," Common Sense Media, October 28, 2013, https://www.commonsensemedia. org/research/zero-to-eight-childrens-media-use-in-america-2013/ key-finding-2%3A-kids%27-time-on-mobile-devices-triples.

24. Sukhbinder Kumar, Katharina von Kriegstein, Karl Friston, Timothy D. Griffiths, "Features versus Feelings: Dissociable Representations of the Acoustic Features and Valence of Aversive Sounds," *Journal of Neuroscience* 32, no. 41 (2012): 14184–14192, doi:10.1523/JNEUROSCI.1759–12.2012.

25. Emma Elliott Freire, "Why I'm Protecting My Baby and Myself from Screen Time," *Federalist*, October 23, 2015, http://thefederal

ist.com/2015/10/23/why-im-protecting-my-baby-and-myself-from
-screen-time/.

26. Alexandra Samuel, "Happy Mother's Day: Kids' Screen Time Is a
Feminist Issue," *JSTOR Daily*, May 3, 2016, https://daily.jstor.org/
screentime-feminist-issue/.

CHAPTER 3

1. The questions were part of a national online general population survey of more than seven hundred adults ages eighteen to fifty-nine.

2. Mizuko Ito, *Engineering Play: A Cultural History of Children's Software*, The John D. and Catherine T. Macarthur Foundation Series
on Digital Media and Learning (Cambridge, MA: MIT Press,
2012), 5.

3. Dimitri Christakis, "When It Comes to Kids, Is All Screen Time
Equal?" National Public Radio, September 11, 2015, video, http://
www.npr.org/2015/09/11/439192407/when-it-comes-to-kids-is-all
-screen-time-equal.

4. Ibid.

5. Natasha Dow Schüll, *Addiction by Design: Machine Gambling in Las
Vegas* (Princeton, NJ: Princeton University Press, 2012), 2.

6. Ibid.

7. Ibid, 41.

8. Mihaly Csikszentmihalyi, "Reflections on Enjoyment," *Perspectives
in Biology and Medicine* 28, no. 4 (1985): 489–97.

9. Schüll, *Addiction by Design*, 171.

10. Ibid., 172.

11. William, "Guiltier Pleasures: Social Cognition in Gaming," *Zang*,
June 20, 2008, https://zang.org/2008/06/20/guiltier-pleasures
-social-cognition-in-gaming/.

12. Ito, *Engineering Play*, 8.

13. Ibid., 9.

14. Erika Christakis, "The New Preschool Is Crushing Kids," *Atlantic*, January/February 2016, https://www.theatlantic.com/magazine/
archive/2016/01/the-new-preschool-is-crushing-kids/419139/.

15. Ibid.

16. "Children Who Enter Kindergarten Late or Repeat Kindergarten:
Their Characteristics and Later School Performance," National
Center for Education Statistics, June 2000, http://nces.ed.gov
/pubs2000/2000039.pdf.

17. T. E. Elder, "The Importance of Relative Standards in ADHD

Diagnoses: Evidence Based on Exact Birth Dates," *Journal of Health Economics* 29, no. 5 (2010): 641–56, https://www.ncbi.nlm.nih.gov /pubmed/20638739?report=abstract.

CHAPTER 4

1. Christopher F. Karpowitz and Jeremy C. Pope, "Summary Report: Marriage and Family—Attitudes, Practices, and Policy Options," The American Family Survey, http://csed.byu.edu/wp-content/ uploads/2016/10/American-Family-Survey_Final-Report.pdf.

2. "Generation M²: Media in the Lives of 8- to 18-Year-Olds," Kaiser Family Foundation, January 2010, https://kaiserfamilyfoundation. files.wordpress.com/2013/04/8010.pdf.

3. Ibid.

4. "Kids & Tech: The Evolution of Today's Digital Natives," Influence Central, 2016, http://influence-central.com/kids-tech -the-evolution-of-todays-digital-natives/.

5. "Transcript: Mayor de Blasio and Chancellor Fariña to Lift School Cell Phone Ban," City of New York official website. http://www1 .nyc.gov/office-of-the-mayor/news/015-15/transcript-mayor-de -blasio-chancellor-fari-a-lift-school-cell-phone-ban.

6. Lisa Sadikman, "Why I Don't Mind When My Teenage Daughter Texts Me from School," *Scary Mommy*, http://www.scarymommy .com/teen-daughter-texts-from-school/.

7. Allison Slater Tate, "I Regret Giving My Children Cellphones, but Not for the Reasons You'd Think," *Washington Post*, April 18, 2016, https://www.washingtonpost.com/news/parenting/wp/2016/04/18 /i-regret-giving-my-children-cell-phones-but-not-for-the-reasons -youd-think/.

8. "The Culture of American Families," Institute for Advanced Studies in Culture, http://iasculture.org/research/culture-formation /culture-american-families.

9. Neetzan Zimmerman, "Louis C.K.'s Explanation of Why He Hates Smartphones Is Sad, Brilliant," *Gawker*, September 20, 2013, http://gawker.com/louis-c-k-s-explanation-of-why-he-hates-smart phones-is-1354954625.

10. Joshua Rhett Miller, "Suicide-Text Girlfriend Has 'No Conscience,' Victim's Mother Says," *New York Post*, June 16, 2017, http://nypost.com/2017/06/16/suicide-text-girlfriend-has -no-conscience-victims-mom-says/.

11. Ibid.

12. Sherry Turkle, *Life on the Screen: Identity in the Age of the Internet* (New York: Simon & Schuster, 1997), 26.

13. Ibid, 61.

14. Brian Christian, "The Samantha Test," *New Yorker*, December 30, 2013, http://www.newyorker.com/culture/culture-desk/the -samantha-test.

15. Sherry Turkle, *Alone Together: Why We Expect More from Technology and Less from Each Other* (New York: Basic Books, 2011), 39.

16. Ibid., 56.

17. Neil Postman, *Amusing Ourselves to Death: Public Discourse in the Age of Show Business* (New York: Penguin, 1985), 77.

18. Leonard Sax, *The Collapse of Parenting: How We Hurt Our Kids When We Treat Them Like Grown-Ups* (New York: Basic Books, 2016), 57.

19. Naomi Schaefer Riley and Christine Rosen, eds., *Acculturated: 23 Savvy Writers Find Hidden Virtue in Reality TV, Chick Lit, Video Games, and Other Pillars of Pop Culture* (West Conshohocken, PA: Templeton Press, 2011), 61–67.

20. Jean M. Twenge, Sara Konrath, Joshua D. Foster, W. Keith Campbell, and Brad J. Bushman, "Egos Inflating Over Time: A Cross-Temporal Meta-Analysis of the Narcissistic Personality Inventory," *Journal of Personality* 76, no. 4 (August 2008): 875–901, https://www .ipearlab.org/media/publications/JoP2008a.pdf.

21. *#Being13: Inside the Secret World of Teens*, CNN, http://www.cnn .com/specials/us/being13.

## CHAPTER 5

1. "Grand Theft Auto V," Common Sense Media, https://www.com monsensemedia.org/game-reviews/grand-theft-auto-v.

2. Sarah Griffiths, "'Grandad' Theft Auto: Middle-Class, Middle-Aged Parents Are Most Likely to Play Violent Crime Game," *Daily Mail*, October 10, 2013, http://www.dailymail.co.uk/sciencetech /article-2451785/Grand-Theft-Auto-Middle-class-middle-aged -parents-likely-play-game.html.

3. D. A. Gentile, D. Li, A. Khoo, S. Prot, and C. A. Anderson, "Mediators and Moderators of Long-Term Effects of Violent Video Games on Aggressive Behavior, Practice, Thinking, and Action," *JAMA Pediatrics* 168, no. 5 (2014): 450–57, doi:10.1001/ jamapediatrics.2014.63.

4. Alice Park, "Little by Little, Violent Video Games Make Us

More Aggressive," *Time*, March 24, 2014, http://time.com/34075/how-violent-video-games-change-kids-attitudes-about-aggression/.

5. Christopher J. Ferguson, "Video Games Don't Make Kids Violent," *Time*, December 7, 2011, http://ideas.time.com/2011/12/07/video-games-dont-make-kids-violent/.

6. Dorothy G. Singer and Jerome L. Singer, *Imagination and Play in the Electronic Age* (Cambridge, MA: Harvard University Press, 2005), 108.

7. Howard Gardner and Katie Davis, *The App Generation: How Today's Youth Navigate Identity, Intimacy, and Imagination in a Digital World* (New Haven, CT: Yale University Press, 2013), 141–42.

8. Ibid., 146.

9. Singer and Singer, *Imagination and Play in the Electronic Age*, 108.

10. Leonard Sax, "Why Do Girls Tend to Have More Anxiety Than Boys?," *New York Times*, April 21, 2016, https://well.blogs.nytimes.com/2016/04/21/why-do-girls-have-more-anxiety-than-boys/.

11. Ibid.

12. Ibid.

13. danah boyd, *It's Complicated: The Social Lives of Networked Teens* (New Haven, CT: Yale University Press, 2014), 13.

14. Andrew K. Przybylski and Victoria Nash, "Internet Filtering Technology and Aversive Online Experiences in Adolescents," *Journal of Pediatrics* 184 (May 2017): 215–19.

15. Libby Plummer, "Do YOU Know What Your Child Is Up to Online? Nearly Half of 10-Year-Olds Say They Have the Technical Skills to Hide Their Activity," *Daily Mail*, October 6, 2016, http://www.dailymail.co.uk/sciencetech/article-3823855/Do-know-child-online-Nearly-half-10-year-olds-say-hide-activity.html.

16. Farhad Manjoo, "'Right to Be Forgotten' Online Could Spread," *New York Times*, August 5, 2015, https://www.nytimes.com/2015/08/06/technology/personaltech/right-to-be-forgotten-online-is-poised-to-spread.html.

17. "Kaplan Test Prep Survey: Percentage of College Admissions Officers Who Check Out Applicants' Social Media Profiles Hits New High; Triggers Include Special Talents, Competitive Sabotage," Kaplan Test Prep, January 13, 2016, http://press.kaptest.com/press-releases/kaplan-test-prep-survey-percentage-of-college-admissions-officers-who-check-out-applicants-social-media-profiles-hits-new-high-triggers-include-special-talents-competitive-sabotage.

18. Ibid.

19. boyd, *It's Complicated*, 58.

20. Ibid., 20.

21. Ibid., 111.

22. Ibid., 74.

23. Martin Daubney, "Experiment That Convinced Me Online Porn Is the Most Pernicious Threat Facing Children Today: By Ex-Lads' Mag Editor Martin Daubney," *Daily Mail*, September 25, 2013, http://www.dailymail.co.uk/femail/article-2432591/Porn-perni cious-threat-facing-children-today-By-ex-lads-mag-editor-MAR TIN-DAUBNEY.html.

24. Nancy Jo Sales, *American Girls: Social Media and the Secret Lives of Teenagers* (New York: Alfred A. Knopf, 2016), 16.

25. Peggy Orenstein, *Girls and Sex: Navigating the Complicated New Landscape* (New York: Harper, 2016), 34.

26. Roni Caryn Rabin, "More Teenage Girls Seeking Genital Cosmetic Surgery," *New York Times*, April 25, 2016, https://well.blogs.nytimes. com/2016/04/25/increase-in-teenage-genital-surgery-prompts-guidelines-for-doctors/.

27. Mark Regnerus and Jeremy Uecker, *Premarital Sex in America* (New York: Oxford University Press, 2011), 97.

28. Ibid., 98.

29. Sales, *American Girls*, 23.

30. Orenstein, *Girls and Sex*, 22.

31. Ibid., 30.

32. Amy Anderson, "Guess What, Feminists? Young Women Pornify Themselves," *Acculturated*, https://acculturated.com/young -women-pornify/.

33. Sales, *American Girls*, 25.

34. Note to Self, "When a School Has a Sexting Scandal," WNYC, November 11, 2015, http://www.wnyc.org/story/why-care-about -sexting/.

35. Hanna Rosin, "Why Kids Sext," *Atlantic*, November 2014, https://www.theatlantic.com/magazine/archive/2014/11/why kids-sext/380798/.

36. Nicole Jacobs and Bill Shields, "Nude Photos of Nearly 50 Duxbury High Teens Found Online," CBS Boston, May 6, 2016, http://boston.cbslocal.com/2016/05/06/nude-photos -duxbury-high-school-police/.

37. Nina Burleigh, "Sexting, Shame, and Suicide: A Shocking Tale of Sexual Assault in the Digital Age," *Rolling Stone*, September 17, 2013, http://www.rollingstone.com/culture/news /sexting-shame-and-suicide-20130917.

38. Amanda Lenhart, Monica Anderson, and Aaron Smith, "Teens,

Technology, and Romantic Relationships," Pew Research Center, October 1, 2015, http://www.pewinternet.org/2015/10/01/teens-technology-and-romantic-relationships/.

39. Sales, *American Girls*, 60.

40. Chuck Hadad, "Why Some 13-Year-Olds Check Social Media 100 Times a Day," CNN, October 13, 2015, http://www.cnn.com/2015/10/05/health/being-13-teens-social-media-study/index.html.

## CHAPTER 6

1. Susan Payne Carter, Kyle Greenberg, and Michael Walker, "Evidence from a Randomized Trial at the United States Military Academy" (working paper, MIT Department of Economics and National Bureau of Economic Research, Cambridge, MA, 2016), https://seii.mit.edu/wp-content/uploads/2016/05/SEII-Discussion-Paper-2016.02-Payne-Carter-Greenberg-and-Walker-2.pdf.

2. Pam A. Mueller and Daniel M. Oppenheimer, "The Pen Is Mightier Than the Keyboard: Advantages of Longhand Over Laptop Note Taking," *Psychological Science* 25, no. 6 (2014), https://sites.udel.edu/victorp/files/2010/11/Psychological-Science-2014-Mueller-0956797614524581-1uohoyu.pdf.

3. Ibid.

4. Cindi May, "A Learning Secret: Don't Take Notes with a Laptop," *Scientific American*, June 3, 2014, https://www.scientificamerican.com/article/a-learning-secret-don-t-take-notes-with-a-laptop/.

5. Charlie Wells, "Look Mom, I'm Writing a Term Paper on My Smartphone," *Wall Street Journal*, February 17, 2016, https://www.wsj.com/articles/look-mom-im-writing-a-term-paper-on-my-smartphone-1455729046.

6. Paul Barnwell, "Do Smartphones Have a Place in the Classroom?," *Atlantic*, April 27, 2016, https://www.theatlantic.com/education/archive/2016/04/do-smartphones-have-a-place-in-the-classroom/480231/.

7. Louis-Philippe Beland and Richard Murphy, "Ill Communication: Technology, Distraction, and Student Performance" (discussion paper, Centre for Economic Performance, London, May 2015), http://cep.lse.ac.uk/pubs/download/dp1350.pdf.

8. Jacob L. Vigdor, Helen F. Ladd, and Erika Martinez, "Scaling the Digital Divide: Home Computer Technology and Student Achievement," *Economic Inquiry* 52, no. 3 (2014): 1103–19.

9. Paul L. Morgan and George Farkas, "Is Special Education Racist?,"

*New York Times*, June 24, 2015, https://www.nytimes.com/2015/06/24
/opinion/is-special-education-racist.html.

10. Center on Media and Human Development, *Children, Media, and Race: Media Use among White, Black, Hispanic, and Asian American Children* (Evanston, IL: Northwestern University, 2011), http://www.blackradionetwork.com/images/userfiles/MediaConsumption.pdf?phpMyAdmin=d8afc5c6e9b6ffb205b5fe3c0c1273fa.

11. "Zero to Eight: Children's Media Use in America," Common Sense Media, Fall 2011, https://webcache.googleusercontent.com/search?q=cache:92iuYWpG9zYJ:https://www.commonsensemedia.org/file/zerotoeightfinal2011pdf-0/download+&cd=2&hl=en&ct=clnk&gl=us.

12. "Mayor de Blasio Announces up to $10 Million Investment in Free Broadband Service for Five NYCHA Developments," NYC, July 16, 2015, http://www1.nyc.gov/office-of-the-mayor/news/491-15/mayor-de-blasio-up-10-million-investment-free-broadband-service-five-nycha#/0.

13. "Bridging the Digital Divide: Library Hot Spot Lending Programs," Urban Libraries Council, June 16, 2015, http://www.urbanlibraries.org/bridging-the-digital-divide--library-hot-spot-lending-programs-event-101.php.

14. Brian Donnelly, "Renovation to Put White Plains Library on the Edge," *White Plains Daily Voice*, October 2, 2012, http://whiteplains.dailyvoice.com/news/renovation-to-put-white-plains-library-on-the-edge/534113/.

15. "Parenting in America," Pew Research Center, December 17, 2015, http://www.pewsocialtrends.org/2015/12/17/parenting-in-america/.

16. Baker, Nicholson. *Substitute: Going to School With a Thousand Kids.* New York, NY: Penguin Books, 2016.

17. Rosalind Wiseman, *Queen Bees and Wannabes*, 3rd ed. (New York: Random House, 2016), 145.

18. Angela Chen, "The Ever-Growing Ed-Tech Market," *Atlantic*, November 6, 2015, https://www.theatlantic.com/education/archive/2015/11/quantifying-classroom-tech-market/414244/.

19. Ibid.

20. Issie Lapowsky, "What Schools Must Learn from LA's iPad Debacle," *Wired*, May 9, 2015, https://www.wired.com/2015/05/los-angeles-edtech/.

21. Chen, "The Ever-Growing Ed-Tech Market."

22. Natasha Singer, "The Silicon Valley Billionaires Remaking America's Schools," *New York Times*, June 6, 2017, https://www.nytimes

.com/2017/06/06/technology/tech-billionaires-education-zucker
berg-facebook-hastings.html.

23. Ibid.

24. Molly Bloom, "Retaking Classes Online: 'Awful If Someone Really Wants to Learn,'" myAJC, October 17, 2016, http:
//www.myajc.com/news/local-education/retaking-classes-on
line-awful-someone-really-wants-learn/WtpYxkN869EqGFN
1mwR2XJ/.

25. Zoë Kirsch, "The New Diploma Mills," *Slate*, May 23, 2017, http://
www.slate.com/articles/news_and_politics/schooled/2017/05/u_s
_high_schools_may_be_over_relying_on_online_credit_recovery_
to_boost.html.

26. Ted Kolderie, *The Split Screen Strategy* (Edina, MN: Beaver's Pond
Press, 2015), 47.

27. Angela Duckworth, *Grit: The Power of Passion and Perseverance*
(New York: Scribner, 2016), 247.

28. Judith Shulevitz, "'Grit,' by Angela Duckworth," *New York Times*,
May 4, 2016, https://www.nytimes.com/2016/05/08/books/review/
grit-by-angela-duckworth.html.

29. Amy Anderson, "Guess What, Feminists? Young Women Pornify
Themselves," April 6, 2016, *Acculturated*, https://acculturated.com
/young-women-pornify/.

30. Ziming Liu, "Reading Behavior in the Digital Environment:
Changes in Reading Behavior over the Past Ten Years," *Journal of Documentation* 61, no. 6 (2005): 700–712, https://doi
.org/10.1108/00220410510632040.

31. Nicholas Carr, *The Shallows: What the Internet Is Doing to Our
Brains* (New York: W.W. Norton, 2011), 16.

32. Charlie Wells, "Look, Mom, I'm Writing a Term Paper on My
Smartphone," *Wall Street Journal*, February 17, 2016, https://www
.wsj.com/articles/look-mom-im-writing-a-term-paper-on-my
-smartphone-1455729046.

33. Verna von Pfetten, "Read This Story Without Distraction (Can
You?)," *New York Times*, May 1, 2016, https://www.nytimes.
com/2016/05/01/fashion/monotasking-drop-everything-and-read
-this-story.html

34. Ibid.

35. Neil Postman, *Amusing Ourselves to Death: Public Discourse in the Age
of Show Business* (New York: Penguin, 1985), 94.

36. Tannis MacBeth Williams, "The Impact of Television: A Natural

Experiment Involving Three Communities," ERIC, 1979, https://eric.ed.gov/?id=ED172293.

37. Carr, *The Shallows*, 65.

38. Kathryn Zickuhr and Lee Rainie, "A Snapshot of Reading in America in 2013," Pew Research Center, January 16, 2014, http://www.pewinternet.org/2014/01/16/a-snapshot-of-reading-in-america-in-2013/.

39. David S. Miall and Teresa Dobson, "Reading Hypertext and the Experience of Literature," *Journal of Digital Information* 2, no. 1 (February 2006).

40. Diane DeStefano and Jo-Anne LeFevre, "Cognitive Load in Hypertext Reading: A Review," *Computers in Human Behavior* 23, no. 3 (2007), http://dl.acm.org/citation.cfm?id=1224003.

41. Arthur Conan Doyle, *A Study in Scarlet & The Sign of the Four* (Hertfordshire, England: Wordsworth Editions Limited, 2007) 12.

42. Torkel Klingberg, *The Overflowing Brain: Information Overload and the Limits of Working Memory* (New York: Oxford University Press, 2008), 36.

43. Carr, *The Shallows*, 192.

44. Alison Flood, "Sharp Decline in Children Reading for Pleasure, Survey Finds," *Guardian*, January 9, 2015, https://www.theguardian.com/books/2015/jan/09/decline-children-reading-pleasure-survey.

45. National Endowment for the Arts, *To Read or Not to Read: A Question of National Consequence* (Washington, DC: National Endowment for the Arts, 2007), https://www.arts.gov/sites/default/files/ToRead.pdf.

46. Flood, "Sharp Decline in Children Reading for Pleasure, Survey Finds."

47. Ibid.

48. Mark Bauerlein, *The Dumbest Generation: How the Digital Age Stupefies Young Americans and Jeopardizes Our Future* (New York: Penguin, 2009), 159.

49. Ibid., 213.

Chapter 7

1. Caitlin Flanagan, "How Helicopter Parenting Can Cause Binge Drinking," *Atlantic*, September 2016, https://www.theatlantic.com/magazine/archive/2016/09/how-helicopter-parents-cause-binge-drinking/492722/.

2. Nicholas Kardaras, *Glow Kids: How Screen Addiction Is Hijacking*

*Our Kids—and How to Break the Trance* (New York: St. Martin's Press, 2016), 66.

3. Ibid., 14.

4. Ibid.

5. Ibid.

6. "Alcohol Facts and Statistics," National Institute on Alcohol Abuse and Alcoholism, February 2017, https://www.niaaa.nih .gov/alcohol-health/overview-alcohol-consumption/alcohol-facts -and-statistics.

7. "Bored and Brilliant Challenge 3: Delete That App," WNYC, February 4, 2015, http://www.wnyc.org/story/challenge-3-delete-app/.

8. Rowena Mason, "MP Nigel Mills Apologises for Playing Candy Crush in Committee Hearing," *Guardian,* (December 8, 2014), https://www.theguardian.com/politics/2014/dec/08/tory-mp-nigel -mills-apologises-candy-crush.

9. V. Joseph Hotz and Juan Pantano, "Strategic Parenting, Birth Order, and School Performance," *Journal of Population Economics* 28, no. 4 (2015): 911–36, https://pdfs.semanticscholar.org/c3bc/428578b701 addbd937d3d0305460a78012ed.pdf.

10. Ibid.

11. Marie Winn, *The Plug-In Drug: Televisions, Computers, and Family Life* (New York: Penguin, 2002), 126.

12. Ibid.

13. Ibid., 128.

14. Dorothy G. Singer and Jerome L. Singer, *Imagination and Play in the Electronic Age* (Cambridge, MA: Harvard University Press, 2005), 22.

15. Ibid.

16. Ibid., 24.

## CHAPTER 8

1. "Crime Statistics," Free-Range Kids, http://www.freerangekids .com/crime-statistics/.

2. Roger S. Ulrich, "View through a Window May Influence Recovery from Surgery," *Science,* 224 (April 27, 1984): 420, https://mdc .mo.gov/sites/default/files/resources/2012/10/ulrich.pdf.

3. Deborah Franklin, "Patients Heal: Hospital Gardens Turn Out to Have Medical Benefits," *Scientific American,* March 1, 2012, https:// www.scientificamerican.com/article/nature-that-nurtures/.

4. Rhonda Clements, "An Investigation of the Status of Outdoor Play," ResearchGate, March 2004, https://www.researchgate.net/

publication/250151481_An_Investigation_of_the_Status_of_Out
door_Play.

5. Don Sabo and Phil Veliz, *Mapping Attrition among U.S. Adolescents
in Competitive, Organized School and Community Sports* (Aspen, CO:
Aspen Institute Project Play, 2014), http://www.dyc.edu/academics/
research/crpash/docs/mapping-attrition-us-sports.pdf

6. Stephen Kaplan, "The Restorative Benefits of Nature: Toward an
Integrative Framework," *Journal of Environmental Psychology*. Vol.
15, Issue 3 (1995): 169–182. 10.1016/0272-4944(95)90001-2.

7. Emily Chertoff, "Reggio Emilia: From Postwar Italy to NYC's Ton-
iest Preschools," *Atlantic*, January 17, 2013, https://www.theatlan
tic.com/national/archive/2013/01/reggio-emilia-from-postwar-italy
-to-nycs-toniest-preschools/267204/.

8. Matt Richtel, "At Waldorf School in Silicon Valley, Technology
Can Wait," *New York Times*, October 22, 2011, http://www.nytimes
.com/2011/10/23/technology/at-waldorf-school-in-silicon-valley
-technology-can-wait.html

9. Ibid.

10. Nick Bilton, "Steve Jobs Was a Low-Tech Parent," *New York Times*,
September 10, 2014, https://www.nytimes.com/2014/09/11/fashion
/steve-jobs-apple-was-a-low-tech-parent.html

11. Yoni Heisler, "Bill Gates Didn't Let His Kids Use Cell Phones until
They Turned 14," *BGR*, April 23, 2017, http://bgr.com/2017/04/23
/bill-gates-kids-cell-phones-rules/.

12. Ibid.

13. Sherry Turkle, *Alone Together: Why We Expect More from Technology
and Less from Each Other* (New York: Basic Books, 2011), xiv.

14. Amanda Lenhart, "A Majority of American Teens Report Access
to a Computer, Game Console, Smartphone, and a Tablet," Pew
Research Center, April 9, 2015, http://www.pewinternet.org/2015
/04/09/a-majority-of-american-teens-report-access-to-a-computer
-game-console-smartphone-and-a-tablet/.

15. Neil Postman, *The Disappearance of Childhood* (New York: Random
House, 1994), 153.

16. Matt Richtel, "No Tie-Ins. No Touch Screens. No Apps.," *New York
Times*, June 8, 2013, http://www.nytimes.com/2013/06/09/business
/at-melissa-doug-toy-company-thriving-on-the-basics.html.

17. Ibid.

18. Jenn Choi, "Toys That Help Kids Become Global Leaders,"
*Quartz*, November 25, 2014, https://qz.com/302023/toys-that-help
-kids-become-global-leaders/.

19. Scott Sampson, *How to Raise a Wild Child: The Art and Science of*

*Falling in Love With Nature* (New York: Houghton Mifflin Harcourt, 2015), 2

20. Elkind, *The Hurried Child*, 221.

21. Rod Dreher, "The Price of Purity," *American Conservative*, April 6, 2016, http://www.theamericanconservative.com/dreher /the-price-of-purity/.

22. Allan Adamson, "Colorado Campaign Wants to Ban Sale of Smartphones for Children Below 13 Years Old," *Tech Times*, June 19, 2017, http://www.techtimes.com/articles/210259/20170619/colorado -campaign-wants-to-ban-sale-of-smartphones-for-children-below -13-years-old.htm.

## Conclusion

1. Nicholas Carr, *The Shallows: What the Internet Is Doing to Our Brains* (New York: W.W. Norton, 2011), 199.

2. Alan Jacobs, "My Year in Tech," *Snakes and Ladders*, December 23, 2015, https://blog.ayjay.org/my-year-in-tech/.

3. Megan Woo, "Hanover Dad Locks Up Daughter's Closet After $500 Phone Bill," NBC12, September 4, 2015, http://www .nbc12.com/story/29962426/hanover-dad-locks-up-daughters -closet-after-500-phone-bill.

4. Neil Postman, *Disappearance of Childhood* (New York: Random House, 1994), 104.

5. Sherry Turkle, *Life on the Screen: Identity in the Age of the Internet* (New York: Simon & Schuster, 1997), 13.

6. Howard Gardner and Katie Davis, *The App Generation: How Today's Youth Navigate Identity, Intimacy, and Imagination in a Digital World* (New Haven, CT: Yale University Press, 2013), 27.

7. Ibid., 78.

8. Marie Winn, *The Plug-In Drug: Televisions, Computers, and Family Life* (New York: Penguin, 2002), 155.

9. Michael Chabon, "Manhood for Amateurs: The Wilderness of Childhood," *New York Review of Books*, July 16, 2009, http://www.ny books.com/articles/2009/07/16/manhood-for-amateurs-the -wilderness-of-childhood/.

10. Ibid.

# Index

....